Lizzie Alldridge

Florence Nightingale, Frances Ridley Havergal, Catherine Marsh, Mrs. Ranyard

Lizzie Alldridge

Florence Nightingale, Frances Ridley Havergal, Catherine Marsh, Mrs. Ranyard

ISBN/EAN: 9783337111847

Printed in Europe, USA, Canada, Australia, Japan

Cover: Foto ©ninafisch / pixelio.de

More available books at **www.hansebooks.com**

THE WORLD'S WORKERS.

Florence Nightingale.
Frances Ridley Havergal.
Catherine Marsh.
Mrs. Ranyard ("L.N.R.").

BY

LIZZIE ALLDRIDGE.

CASSELL & COMPANY, Limited:
LONDON, PARIS, NEW YORK, & MELBOURNE.
1885.
[ALL RIGHTS RESERVED.]

CONTENTS.

	PAGE
Florence Nightingale	5
Frances Ridley Havergal	35
Catherine Marsh	65
Mrs. Ranyard ("L.N.R.")	99

FLORENCE NIGHTINGALE.

EVERYONE who knows London at all knows the Houses of Parliament at the foot of Westminster Bridge. Across the bridge on the Surrey bank, just opposite the great Gothic Houses where legislators talk and govern, stands the new St. Thomas's Hospital, where sick folk suffer, get cured, or die; where young doctors "walk," and older ones teach; where experienced nurses tend the sick, and where probationers are trained.

Let us go over the crowded bridge, through the long corridors of the hospital, and enter a large room, where tables are neatly laid for a numerous company, and there look at a statuette under a glass shade on a pedestal. There she stands, a ministering woman. Her dress is the simple garb of common life, as it was in the days of the Crimean War, with no separating badge to mark her off from her fellow-beings. In one hand she holds a nurse's night-lamp, with the other she shades the light from the eyes of the sick faces she is watching. You do not see their faces, but you know that *she* sees them; on every line of hers you read how carefully and wisely, and with what clear knowledge and gentle womanliness she is pondering what she sees.

It is a statuette of Florence Nightingale. It stands in the dining-room of the Nightingale Home, St. Thomas's Hospital; where those who have eyes and hearts and brains may study it, and learn the lessons taught with such quiet, unobtrusive force.

That Nightingale Home is part of the British nation's tribute of thanks to the noble woman who found the death-rate in the Barrack Hospital at Scutari 60 per cent., and left it a fraction over 1.

The Nightingale Home is established for the purpose of training nurses. Two classes of women are admitted: those who are termed "nurse probationers;" and gentlewomen, who are "special probationers."

A very distinguished lady nurse who has been in half the hospitals in Europe once said to me, "To Florence Nightingale, who was my own first teacher and inspirer, we owe the wonderful change that has taken place in the public mind with regard to nursing. When I first began my hospital training, hospital nursing was thought to be a profession which no decent woman of any rank could follow. If a servant turned nurse, it was supposed she did so because she had lost her character. We have changed all that now. Modern nursing owes its first impulse to Florence Nightingale."

I don't suppose that any of my young readers have ever seen a hospital nurse of the now nearly extinct Gamp type; but I have. I have seen her, coarse-faced, thick of limb, heavy of foot, brutal in speech, crawling up and down the stairs or about the wards in dresses and aprons that made me feel (although quite well and with a good healthy appetite) as if I would rather not have my dinner just then. These were the old-fashioned " Sairey Gamps." But Florence Nightingale has been too strong for even the immortal " Sairey." Go now through the corridors and wards of a modern hospital ; every nurse you meet will be neat and trim with spotless dress and cap and apron, moving quietly but quickly to and fro, doing her work with kindness and intelligence.

The Nightingale Home itself is charming ; and many, were they to see the little white beds and pleasant rooms of the probationers, or were to stand at the windows of the wards, overlooking the busy Thames and the opposite Houses of Parliament, or to meet the probationers trooping down to dinner, some in their soft grey alpacas, which tell they have just come from the lecture-room, and others, in print gowns and white aprons, from the wards, would desire to become " Nightingales." But this is no easy matter : no one is admitted before twenty-three years of age ; the preliminary training is very thorough, and they have to work very hard; most of them find it trying at first; indeed, every woman must be sure of her vocation before she attempts the work, interesting as it is to those who care for it in the highest spirit.

It was in 1820, the year George the Third's long life quite faded out, that the younger of the two daughters of William Shore Nightingale was born at Florence, and named after that lovely city.

Mr. Nightingale, of Embley Park, Hampshire, and the Lea Hurst, Derbyshire, was a very wealthy landowner. He was of the Shores of Derbyshire, but inherited the fortune with the name of Nightingale through his mother. Lea Hurst, where Miss Nightingale passed the summer months of each year, is situated in the Matlock district, among bold masses of limestone rock, gray walls, full of fossils, covered with moss and lichen, with the changeful river Derwent now dashing over its stony bed, now quietly winding between little dales with clefts and dingles. Those who have travelled by the Derby and Buxton railway will remember the narrow valleys, the mountain streams, the wide spans of high moorland, the distant ranges of hills beyond hills of the district. Lea Hurst, a gable-ended house, standing among its own woods and commanding wonderful views of the Peak country, is about two miles from Cromford station.

At Lea Hurst much of Florence Nightingale's

childhood was passed. There she early developed that intense love for every living suffering thing that grew with her growth, until it became the master-passion of her life.

A few years since a true story of her as a little girl appeared in *Little Folks* Magazine, and it is so charmingly told, and gives so distinctly the key-note of her character, that I repeat it here in full, as to curtail it would be to spoil it :—

Some years ago, when the celebrated Florence Nightingale was a little girl, living at her father's home, a large, old Elizabethan house with great woods about it, in Hampshire, there was one thing that struck everybody who knew her. It was that she seemed to be always thinking what she could do to please or help any one who needed either help or comfort. She was very fond, too, of animals, and she was so gentle in her way, that even the shyest of them would come quite close to her, and pick up whatever she flung down for them to eat. There was, in the garden behind the house, a long walk with trees on each side, the abode of many squirrels; and when Florence came down the walk, dropping nuts as she went along, the squirrels would run down the trunks of their trees, and hardly waiting until she passed by, would pick up the prize, and dart away with their little bushy tails curled over their backs, and their black eyes looking about as if terrified at the least noise, though they did not seem to be afraid of Florence. The reason was that she loved them, and never did anything to startle or trouble them.

Then there was an old grey pony, named Peggy, past work, living in a paddock, with nothing to do all day long but to amuse herself. Whenever Florence appeared at the gate, Peggy would come trotting up and put her nose into the dress pocket of her little mistress, and pick it of the apple or the roll of bread that she knew she would always find there, for this was a trick Florence had taught the pony. Florence was fond of riding, and her father's old friend (the clergyman of the parish) used often to come and take her for a ride with him when he went to the farm cottages at a distance. He was a good man, and very kind to the poor. As he had studied medicine when a young man, he was able to tell the people what would do them good when they were ill, or had met with an accident. Little Florence took great delight in helping to nurse those who were ill, and whenever she went on these long rides, she had a small basket fastened to her saddle, filled with something nice, which she had saved from her breakfast or dinner, or carried for her mother, who was very good to the poor. She thus learned to be useful as well as kind-hearted.

Now, there lived in one of two or three solitary cottages in the wood, an old shepherd of her father's, named Roger, who had a favourite sheep-dog called Cap. Roger had neither wife nor child, and Cap lived with him, and kept him company at nights, after he had penned his flock. Cap was a very sensible dog; indeed, people used to say he "could do everything but speak." He kept the sheep in wonderfully good order, and thus saved his master a great deal of trouble. One day as Florence and her old friend were out for a ride, they came to a field, where they found the shepherd giving his sheep their night feed; but he was without the dog, and the sheep knew it, for they were scampering about in all directions. Florence and her friend noticed that the old shepherd looked very sad this evening, and they stopped to ask what was the matter, and what had become of his dog.

"Oh," said Roger, "Cap will never be of any more use to me; I'll have to hang him, poor fellow, as soon as I go home to night."

"Hang him!" said Florence. "Oh, Roger, how wicked of you! What has dear old Cap done?"

"He has done nothing," replied Roger; "but he will never be of any more use to me, and I cannot afford to keep him for nothing; one of the mischievous schoolboys throwed a stone at him yesterday, and broke one of his legs." And the old shepherd's eyes filled with tears, which he wiped away with his shirt-sleeve; then he drove his spade deep in the ground to hide what he felt, for he did not like to be seen crying.

"Poor Cap!" he sighed, "he was as knowing as a human being almost."

"But are you sure his leg is broken?" asked Florence.

"Oh, yes, miss, it is broken safe enough; he has not put his foot to the ground since."

Florence and her friend rode on without saying anything more to Roger.

"We will go and see poor Cap," said the vicar. "I don't believe the leg is really broken. It would take a big stone, and a hard blow, to break the leg of a great dog like Cap."

"Oh, if you could but cure him, how glad Roger would be!" replied Florence.

They soon reached the shepherd's cottage; but the door was fastened, and when they moved the latch such a furious barking was heard, that they drew back startled. However, a little boy came out of the next cottage, and asked if they wanted to go in, as Roger had left the key with his mother. So the key was got, and the door opened, and there on the bare brick floor lay the dog, his hair dishevelled, and his eyes sparkling with anger at the intruders. But when he saw the little boy he grew pacified. Dogs always know their friends. And when he looked at Florence, and heard her call him "poor Cap," he began to wag his short tail, and then crept from under the table, and lay down at her feet. She took hold of one of his paws, patted his old rough head, and talked to him, whilst her friend examined the injured leg. It was dreadfully swollen, and hurt him very much to have it examined; but the dog knew it was meant kindly, and though he moaned and winced with pain, he licked the hands that were hurting him.

"It's only a bad bruise; no bones are broken," said her old friend; "rest is all Cap needs; he will soon be well again."

"I am so glad," exclaimed Florence; "but can we do nothing for him? he seems in such pain."

"There is one thing that would ease the pain, and heal the leg all the sooner, and that is plenty of hot water to foment the part."

"Well then," said Florence, "if that will do him good, I will foment poor Cap's leg."

"I fear you will only scald yourself," replied he.

But Florence had in the meantime struck a light with the tinder-box, and lighted the fire, which was already laid. She then set off to the other cottage to get something to bathe the leg with. She found an old flannel petticoat hanging up to dry, and this she carried off, and tore up into slips, which she wrung out in warm water, and laid them tenderly on Cap's swollen leg. It was not long before the poor dog felt the benefit of the application, and he looked grateful, wagging his little stump of a tail in thanks. On their way home they met the shepherd coming slowly along, with a piece of rope in his hand.

"Oh, Roger," cried Florence, "you are not to hang poor old Cap; his leg is not broken at all."

"No, he will serve you yet," said the vicar.

"Well, I be main glad to hear it," said the shepherd, "and many thanks to you for going to see him."

On the next morning Florence was up early, and the first thing she did was to take two flannel petticoats to give the poor woman whose petticoat she had torn up to bathe Cap. Then she went to the dog, and was delighted to find the swelling of his leg much less. She bathed it again, and Cap was as grateful as before.

Two or three days afterwards Florence and her friend were riding together, when they came up to Roger and his sheep. This time Cap was watching the sheep, though he was lying quite still, and pretending to be asleep. When he heard the voice of Florence speaking to his master, who was portioning out the usual feed, his tail wagged and his eyes sparkled, but he did not get up, for he was on duty. The shepherd stopped his work, and as he glanced at the dog with a merry laugh, said, "Do look at the dog, miss; he be so pleased to hear your voice." Cap's tail went faster and faster. "I be glad," continued the old man, "I did not hang him. I be greatly obliged to you, miss, and the vicar, for what you did. But for you I would have hanged the best dog I ever had in my life."

Florence Nightingale always retained her belief in animals. Many years afterwards, when her name was known all over the world, she wrote: "A small pet animal is often an excellent companion for the sick, for long chronic cases especially. An invalid, in giving an account of his nursing by a nurse and a dog, infinitely preferred that of the dog. "Above all," he said, "it did not talk." Even Florence Nightingale's maimed dolls were tenderly nursed and bandaged.

Mr. Nightingale was a man singularly in advance of his time as regards the training of girls. The "higher education of women," was unknown to the general public in those days, but not to Mr. Nightingale. His daughter was taught mathematics, and studied the classics, history, and modern languages, under her father's guidance. These last were afterwards of the greatest use to her in the Crimea. But she was no "learned lady;" only a well-educated Englishwoman, all round. She was an excellent musician, and skilful in work with the needle; and the delicate trained touch thus acquired stood her in good stead, for the soldiers used to say that a wound which Miss Nightingale dressed "was sure to get well."

She felt a strong craving for work, more even than the schools and cottages, the care of the young, the sick, and the aged (in which she followed her mother's example) could afford her at her father's home.

Mrs. Browning tells us to

> "Get leave to work
> In this world; 'tis the best you get at all."

Florence Nightingale not only got leave to work, but did so, very quietly but very persistently. And so she became a pioneer for less courageous souls, and won for them also "leave to work." Taught by her father, she soon learned to distinguish between what was really good work and which mere make-believe. She had many opportunities even as a child of seeing really fine, artistic work both in science and art. She set up a high standard, and was never satisfied with anything short of the best, either in herself or others. It is a grand thing to know good work when you see it.

The love of work, however, with Florence Nightingale always went hand in hand with that love for every living thing in God's world, which was born with her, and which was never crowded out by all this education. As she grew up she more and more felt that helpfulness was the first law of her being; but her reason and intellect having been so carefully trained, she was thoroughly persuaded that in order to help effectually, one must know thoroughly both the cause of suffering and its radical cure.

The study of nursing had an irresistible attraction for her. Few people in England at that time valued nursing. Florence Nightingale was convinced that indifference arose from the all but absolute ignorance of what nursing should be, and she set herself to acquire the necessary knowledge to enable her to carry it out in the very best and most scientific way. She never lost an opportunity of visiting a hospital either at home or abroad. She gave up the life of so-called "pleasure" which it was then considered a young woman of her position ought to lead, and after having very carefully examined innumerable nursing institutions at home and abroad, at length went to the well-known Pastor Fliedner's Deaconesses at Kaiserswerth, where she remained for several months.

When "Sweet Agnes Jones," who was at one time a "Nightingale" probationer at St. Thomas's, was learning to nurse at Kaiserswerth several years later, she found that Florence Nightingale was tenderly remembered there, not only for her wonderful skill, but for the earnestness with which she had tried to win the souls of her sick people to Christ.

After leaving Kaiserswerth, Miss Nightingale was for a while with the Sisters of St. Vincent de Paul in Paris, so anxious was she to see how nursing was carried on under many different systems. It was during 1851, the year of the first Great Exhibition, that she was thus fitting herself practically for the great task that lay before her in the not very distant future.

On her return to England, Miss Nightingale found a patient that required all her time and help of every kind. This patient was none other than the Sanatorium in Harley Street for gentlewomen of limited means. Into the saving of this valuable institution Miss Nightingale threw all her energy, and for two or three years, hidden away from the outside world, she was working day and night for her poor suffering ladies, until at length she was able to feel that the Sanatorium was not only in good health but on the high road to permanent success.

Florence Nightingale's own health, however, gave way under the long-continued strain of anxiety and fatigue; she was obliged to leave the invalids for whom she had done so much, and go home for the rest and change she so sorely needed.

Now, while Miss Nightingale had been quietly getting "Harley Street" into working order, the gravest and most terrible changes had taken place in the affairs of the nation, and not only in those of England, but in those of the whole of Europe.

In 1851, when the first Great Exhibition was opened, all was peace—the long peace of forty years was still unbroken, people said it never was to be broken again, and that wars and rumours of wars had come to an end. So much for human foreknowledge. By the autumn of 1854, the horrors of the Crimean war had reached their climax. The *Times* was full, day by day, of the most thrilling and appalling descriptions of the hideous sufferings of our brave men, sufferings caused quite as much by the utter breakdown of the sanitary administration as by even the deadly battles and trench-work; while every post was bringing agonising private letters appealing for help.

Men were wounded in the Crimea, the hospitals were far off at Scutari, the wide and stormy Black Sea had to be crossed to reach them; the stores of food, clothing, and medicine that might have saved many a life were at Varna, or lost in the *Black Prince;* the state of the great Barrack Hospital at Scutari was indescribably horrible; everybody was frantic to rush to the relief; no one knew what best to do; public feeling was at fever-heat. How could it be otherwise when William Howard Russell, the *Times* correspondent, was constantly writing such true but heartrending letters as this?—

"The commonest accessories of a hospital are wanting; there is not the least attention paid to decency or cleanliness; the stench is appalling; the fœtid air can barely struggle out to taint the atmosphere, save through the chinks in the walls and roofs; and, for all I can observe, these men die without the least effort being made to save them. There they lie, just as they were let gently down on the ground by the poor fellows, their comrades, who brought them on their backs from the camp with the greatest tenderness, but who are not allowed to remain with them.

The sick appear to be tended by the sick, and the dying by the dying."

Miss Nightingale, who was then recovering from her Harley Street nursing, deeply felt the intensity of the crisis that was moving the whole nation; but, whereas the panic had driven most of the kind people who were so eager to help the army nearly "off their heads," it only made hers the cooler and clearer. She wrote offering her services to Mr. Sidney Herbert, afterwards Lord Herbert, the Minister for War, who, together with his wife, had long known her, and had recognised her wonderful organising faculties, and her great practical experience.

It was on the 15th of October that she wrote to Mr. Herbert. On the very same day the Minister had written to her. Their letters crossed. Mr. Herbert, who had himself given much attention to military hospitals, laid before Miss Nightingale, in his now historical letter, a plan for nursing the sick and wounded at Scutari.

"There is, as far as I know," he wrote, "only one person in England capable of organising and directing such a plan, and I have been several times on the point of asking you if you would be disposed to make the attempt. That it will be difficult to form a corps of nurses, no one knows better than yourself."

After specifying the difficulty in finding not only good nurses, but good nurses who *would be willing to submit to authority*, he goes on, "I have this simple question to put to you. Could you go out yourself and take charge of everything? It is, of course, understood that you will have absolute authority over all the nurses, unlimited power to draw on the Government for all you judge necessary to the success of your mission; and I think I may assure you of the cooperation of the medical staff. Your personal qualities, your knowledge, and your authority in administrative affairs all fit you for this position."

Miss Nightingale at once concurred in Mr. Herbert's proposal. The materials for a staff of good nurses did not exist, and she had to put up with the best that could be gathered on such short notice.

On the 21st, a letter by Mr. Herbert from the War Office told the world that "Miss Nightingale, accompanied by thirty-four nurses, will leave this evening. Miss Nightingale, who has, I believe, greater practical experience of hospital administration and treatment than any other lady in this country, has, with a self-devotion for which I have no words to express my gratitude, undertaken this noble but arduous work."

A couple of days later there was a paragraph in the *Times* from Miss Nightingale herself, referring to the gifts for the soldiers that had been offered so lavishly: "Miss Nightingale neither invites nor refuses the generous offers. Her banking account is open at Messrs. Coutts'." On the 30th of October, the *Times* republished from the *Examiner* a letter, headed "Who is Miss Nightingale?" and signed "One who has known her." Then was made known to the British public for the first time who the woman that had gone to the aid of the sick and wounded really was; then it was shown that she was no hospital matron, but a young and singularly graceful and accomplished gentlewoman of wealth and position, who had, not in a moment of national enthusiasm, but as the set purpose of her life from girlhood up, devoted herself to the studying of God's great and good laws of health, and to trying to apply them to the help of her suffering fellow-creatures.

From that 30th of October, 1854, the heroine of the Crimean war was Florence Nightingale, and the heroine of that war will she be while the English tongue exists, and English history is read. The national enthusiasm for her was at once intense; and it grew deeper and more intense as week by week revealed her powers. "Less talent and energy of character, less singleness of purpose and devotion, could never have combined the heterogeneous elements which she gathered together in one common work and labour of love."

I met, the other day, a lady who saw something of Miss Nightingale just before she went out to the East. This lady tells me that Miss Nightingale was then most graceful in appearance, tall and slight, very quiet and still. At first sight her earnest face struck one as cold; but when she began to speak she grew very animated, and her dark eyes shone out with a peculiarly star-like brightness.

This was the woman whose starting for the East was at once felt to be the beginning of better things; but so prejudiced were many good English people against women-nurses for soldiers that Mrs. Jameson, writing at the time, calls the scheme "an undertaking wholly new to our English customs, much at variance with the usual education given to women in this country." She, sensible woman, one in advance of her day, hoped it would succeed, but hoped rather faintly. "If it succeeds," she goes on, "it will be the true, the lasting glory of Florence Nightingale, and her band of devoted assistants, that they have broken down a 'Chinese wall of prejudices,' religious, social, professional, and have established a precedent which will, indeed, multiply the good to all time."

The little band of nurses crossed the channel to Boulogne, where they found the fisherwomen eager for the honour of carrying their luggage to the railway. This display, however, seemed to Miss Nightingale to be so out of keeping with the deep gravity of her mission, that, at her wish, it was not repeated at any of the stopping-places during the route. The *Vectis* took the nurses across the Mediterranean, and a terribly rough passage they had. On Nov. 5th, the very day on which the battle of Inkermann was fought, the ship arrived at Scutari.

Miss Nightingale and her nurses landed during the afternoon, and it was remarked at the time that their neat black dresses formed a strong contrast to those of the usual hospital attendants. A large number of men, wounded at Balaclava, had been landed the day before.

The great Barrack Hospital at Scutari, which had been lent to the British by the Turkish Government, was an enormous quadrangular building, a quarter of a mile each way, with square towers at each angle. It stood on the Asiatic shore a hundred feet above the Bosphorus. Another large hospital stood near; the whole, at times, containing as many as four thousand men. The whole were placed under Miss Nightingale's care. The nurses were lodged in the south-east tower.

The extent of corridors in the great hospital, storey above storey, in which the sick and wounded were at first laid on wretched palliasses as close together as they could be placed, made her inspection and care most difficult. There were two rows of mattresses in the corridors, where two persons could hardly pass abreast between foot and foot. The mortality, when the *Times* first took up the cause of the sick and wounded, was enormous.

In the Crimea itself there was not half the mortality in the tents, horrible as were the sufferings and privations of the men there.

"The whole of yesterday," writes one of the nurses a few days after they had arrived, "one could only forget one's own existence, for it was spent, first in sewing the men's mattresses together, and then in washing them and assisting the surgeons, when we could, in dressing their ghastly wounds after their five days' confinement on board ship, during which space their wounds had not been dressed. Hundreds of men with fever, dysentery, and cholera (the wounded were the smaller portion) filled the wards in succession, from the overcrowded transports."

Miss Nightingale's position was a most difficult one. Everything was in disorder, and every official was extremely jealous of interference. Miss Nightingale, however, at once impressed upon her staff the duty of obeying the doctors' orders, as she did herself. An invalid's kitchen was established immediately by her to supplement the rations. A laundry was added ; the nursing itself was, however, the most difficult and important part of the work.

But it would take far too much space to give all the details of that kind but strict administration which brought comparative comfort and a low death-rate into the Scutari hospitals. During a year and a-half the labour of getting the hospitals into working order was enormous, but before the Peace arrived they were models of what such institutions may be.

Speaking of Miss Nightingale in the Hospital at Scutari, the *Times* correspondent wrote: "Wherever there is disease in its most dangerous form, and the hand of the spoiler distressingly nigh, there is that incomparable woman sure to be seen; her benignant presence is an influence for good comfort even amid the struggles of expiring nature. She is a 'ministering angel,' without any exaggeration, in these hospitals, and as her slender form glides quietly along each corridor, every poor fellow's face softens with gratitude at the sight of her. When all the medical officers have retired for the night, and silence and darkness have settled down upon these miles of prostrate sick, she may be observed, alone, with a little lamp in her hand, making her solitary rounds. With the heart of a true woman and the manner of a lady, accomplished and refined beyond most of her sex, she combines a surprising calmness of judgment and promptitude and decision of character. The popular instinct was not mistaken, which, when she set out from England on her mission of mercy, hailed her as a heroine; I trust that she may not earn her title to a higher, though sadder, appellation. No one who has observed her fragile figure and delicate health can avoid misgivings lest these should fail."

Public feeling bubbled up into poetry. Even doggrel ballads sung about the streets praised

"The Nightingale of the East,
For her heart it means good."

Among many others, the American poet, Longfellow, wrote the charming poem, *The Lady with the Lamp*, so beautifully illustrated by the statuette of Florence Nightingale at St. Thomas's Hospital, suggested by the well-known incident recorded in a soldier's letter:

"She would speak to one and another, and nod and smile to many more; but she could not do it to all, you know, for we lay there by hundreds; but we could kiss her shadow as it fell, and lay our heads on our pillows again content."

> "Lo! in that house of misery
> A lady with a lamp I see
>   Pass through the glimmering gloom,
>   And flit from room to room.
>
> "And slow, as in a dream of bliss,
> The speechless sufferer turns to kiss
>   Her shadow as it falls
>   Upon the darkening walls.
>
> "On England's annals, through the long
> Hereafter of her speech and song,
>   A light its rays shall cast
>   From portals of the past.
>
> "A lady with a lamp shall stand
> In the great history of the land,
>   A noble type of good,
>   Heroic womanhood."

In the following spring Miss Nightingale crossed the Black Sea and visited Balaclava, where the state of the hospitals in huts was extremely distressing, as help of all kinds was even more difficult to obtain there than at Scutari. Here Miss Nightingale spent some weeks, until she was prostrated by a severe attack of the Crimean fever, of which she very nearly died.

The characteristic little extract following will show at once her power of observation, and how readily she turns every scrap of personal experience to advantage for other sufferers:

"I have seen in fevers (and felt when I was a fever patient myself in the Crimea) the most acute suffering produced from the patient (in a hut) not being able to see out of window, and the knots in the wood being the only view. I shall never forget the rapture of fever patients over a bunch of bright-coloured flowers. I remember (in my own case) a nosegay of wild flowers being sent me, and from that moment recovery becoming more rapid."

But at length the Crimean War came to an end. The nation was prepared to welcome its heroine with the most passionate enthusiasm. But Florence Nightingale quietly slipped back unnoticed to her Derbyshire home, without its being known that she had passed through London.

Worn out with ill-health and fatigue, and naturally shrinking from publicity, the public at large has scarcely ever seen her; she has been a great invalid ever since the war, and for many years hardly ever left her house.

But her energy has been untiring. She was one of the founders of the Red Cross Society for the relief of the sick and wounded in war. When the Civil War broke out in America she was consulted as to all the details of the military nursing there. "Her name is almost more known amongst us than even in Europe," wrote an American. During the Franco-German War she gave advice for the chief hospitals under the Crown Princess, the Princess Alice, and others. The Children's Hospital at Lisbon was erected from her plans. The hospitals in Australia, India, and other places, have received her care. A large proportion of the plans for the building and organisation of the hospitals erected during the last twenty-five years in England have passed through her hands.

The Queen, who had followed her work with constant interest, presented her with a beautiful and costly decoration. The nation gave £50,000 to found the Nightingale Home.

In this home Miss Nightingale takes the deepest interest, constantly having the nurses and sisters to visit her, and learning from them the most minute details of its working. Great is evidently her rejoicing when one of her "Nightingales" proves to be a really fine nurse, such a one, for instance, as Agnes Jones, the reformer of workhouse nursing.

When Agnes Jones died in 1868, Miss Nightingale broke through her retirement in an article in a monthly magazine, called "Una and her Lions," a sketch, indeed, of her friend's taming the paupers, but far more is it a portrait of Florence Nightingale by herself. This article now forms the introduction of the well-known memorials of Agnes Jones. It is a noble tribute from one great worker to another. It throws so much light on the true character of Florence Nightingale herself; it brings you closely into contact with her own heart and brain, that you feel as you read it she must be writing her own experience. A true portrait of herself by herself comes out when we look at that record as a whole. You see how Florence Nightingale herself had to fight, first against the people who thought nursing as a profession unfit for decent women, then with those who admitted it might be followed by "the lower middle-class," and lastly with those who considered it a natural gift, for which no training at all was necessary.

Just notice the strong terseness, the business-like pointedness, as well as the beautiful earnestness, both religious and artistic, of the following. After telling us of the wonders wrought by Una on her paupers, more hard to tame than lions, she goes on: "In less than three years she did this. And how did she do all this?"

"Agnes had trained herself to the utmost; she was always training herself; for nursing is no holiday work. Nursing is an art; and, if it is to be made an art, requires as exclusive a devotion, as hard a preparation.

as any painter's or sculptor's work; for what is the having to do with dead canvas or cold marble compared with having to do with the living body, the temple of God's Spirit? Nursing is one of the Fine Arts; I had almost said, the finest of the Fine Arts."

"Fid-fadding" was one of the besetting sins of most women in the days when Florence Nightingale was young. It was certainly one of the sins most abhorrent to her energetic nature. "How can any undervalue business habits? As if anything could be done without them!" she exclaims.

This was the high position Florence Nightingale conquered for her fellow-women. Hundreds have occupied, and are still occupying, the ground she won for them. "And I give a quarter of a century's European experience," she goes on, " when I say that the happiest people, the fondest of their occupation, the most thankful for their lives, are in my opinion those engaged in sick nursing."

I will quote no more, but if you really want to know Florence Nightingale, read the Introduction to "Agnes Jones," which shows that Miss Nightingale has as great a power of administrating pen and ink as hospitals. Her invalid life since the war has been full of business; the amount of work of all kinds, at home and abroad, she has done since the war is enormous. "Notes on Nursing," an invaluable book which the *Medical Times* declared no one else could have written, has entirely conquered the bad old ideas, and has shown what an art and science nursing can become; better still, it has "vindicated the ways of God with man." "Notes on Hospitals," less well known to the general public, contains a perfect mine of information, the gist of which she has reduced, in a most marvellous appendix, under five simple headings. A few remarks from the preface of the third edition will show with what patient care she had thought out the subject.

"It may seem a strange principle to enunciate as the very first requirement in a hospital, that it should do the sick no harm. It is quite necessary, nevertheless, to lay down such a principle, because the actual mortality *in* hospitals, especially in those of large crowded cities, is very much higher than any calculation founded on the mortality of the same class of diseases among patients treated out of hospital would lead us to expect. *The knowledge of this fact first induced me to examine into the influence exercised by hospital construction on the duration and death-rate of cases received into the wards.*"

Officials in high places, ever since the Crimean War, have sent Miss Nightingale piles, mountains, one might say, of Reports and Blue Books for her advice. She seems to be able to condense any number of them into half-a-dozen telling sentences; for instance, the mortality in Indian regiments during times of peace became exceedingly alarming. Reports on the subject were poured in upon her.

"The men are simply treated like Strasbourg geese," she said in effect. "They eat, sleep, frizzle in the sun, and eat and sleep again. Treat them reasonably, and they will be well."

She has written much valuable advice on "How to live and not die in India."

Children's Hospitals have also engaged much of her attention. You cannot open one of her books at hazard without being struck with some shrewd remark that tells how far-reaching is her observation; as in this, on the playgrounds of Children's Hospitals: "A large garden-ground, laid out in sward and grass hillocks, and such ways as children like (not too pretty, or the children will be scolded for spoiling it) must be provided."

Here, I am sorry to find, my space comes to an end, but not, I hope, before I have been able to sketch in some slight way what great results will assuredly follow when Faith and Science are united in one person. In the days which we may hope are now dawning, when these gifts will be united, not in an individual here and there, but in a large portion of our race, there will doubtless be many a devoted woman whose knowledge may equal her practical skill and her love for God and her fellow-creatures, who will understand, even more thoroughly than most of us now can (most of us being still so ignorant), how deep a debt of gratitude is due to her who first opened for women so many paths of duty, and raised nursing from a menial employment to the dignity of an "Art of Charity"—to England's first great nurse, the wise, beloved, and far-seeing heroine of the Crimean War, the Lady of the Lamp, Florence Nightingale.

FRANCES RIDLEY HAVERGAL.

THE story of Frances Ridley Havergal's life is the history of the growth of love to Christ in her own soul. In the simple records of herself and her nearest relatives this growth has been so clearly placed before us that we are able to trace it from its first stirrings in her childish heart right up to the moment when, her dying face lighted with heavenly radiance, her earthly voice failed for ever as she saw her King in His beauty in the land

"Where all His singers meet."

To Frances Ridley Havergal was given not only to feel in a most wonderful degree that ecstatic love to Christ and entire consecration to Him, which are such marked and blessed characteristics of much of the Christian life of the present day, but an almost unique power of so expressing that love that wherever an English book can be read, there hearts have felt the glow of her devotion. In her case the love came slowly, and so did the power of pouring it out. Her alabaster box of precious ointment was long in filling; but when it was filled, with what rapture did she break it at the blessed feet of her King!

Frances Ridley Havergal was born at the end of the year 1836. She was the sixth and youngest child of the Rev. Henry Havergal and of Jane his wife. Her father was at that time Rector of Astley, Worcestershire. He and his wife were both very earnest, spiritually-minded, evangelical Christians; and their home was rich in all holy influences, in much beauty, and in a delightful musicalness. Mr. Havergal was, indeed, "a living song," filling the house with holy melodies, and his wife a most lovely woman. The last baby, Frances, shared the happy fate of most last babies; she was the special pet of the family, and seems to have been designed by nature for that position. At two years old she was a very fairy-like creature, with light curling hair, bright expression, and a most fair complexion. A prettier child, writes her elder sister, Miriam, was seldom seen. Much of this sunny fairness and brightness she kept throughout her life.

At two years of age she could speak with perfect distinctness. This easy command of language grew with her growth, and is very noticeable in her books. Like all other young children, she liked to have stories told her, and was very fond of animals, especially of a certain Flora or Flo, a beautiful white-and-tan spaniel, who was her great friend and companion. This love of animals never left her. Many years afterwards she wrote: "Guess my birthday treat? To the Zoological Gardens. I don't know anything I would rather see in London."

At a very early age Frances picked up a good bit of knowledge without much trouble to herself. At morning prayers she always sat on her father's knee whilst he read the Scriptures, and from him she learned to sing hymns very sweetly. When she was three she could read easy books, and was often found hidden under a table with some engrossing story.

On her third birthday she was crowned with a wreath of pink China roses, which Miriam made for her, and on her fourth birthday she was brought down to dessert garlanded with bay leaves; and a most lovely little picture she made, with her exquisite fairness, and her bright sparkling eyes full of merriment. At four Frances could read the Bible, but great care was always taken not to tire her, or to excite the precocity of her mind.

The little maiden was, however, so fond of learning that she could not be kept from it. For instance, while the others were having their German lesson, she would take care to be in the room, and without any one's knowing that she was listening, picked up so much that the master begged to be allowed to teach her.

Rhymes came naturally to her. Her father was a great composer of hymn tunes and sacred poetry, and music filled the atmosphere in which she lived.

At that early age she had a little book in which she did a great deal of scribbling, mostly in rhyme. Her sister Miriam married, and when Frances was promoted to the dignity of aunt she wrote a copybook full of simple tales for her little niece.

From nine years old she wrote long and amusing letters to her brother Frank and her young friends. In fact, it seems she took to her pen quite naturally; and writing, in those early days, does not seem to have been any trouble to her. Indeed, to those who saw only her outward life, Frances, in her early childhood, was a very merry little girl, much given to sitting up in trees and climbing walls; though the poor child had one very great trouble in her heart, which she carefully hid away even from the most loving eyes.

Perhaps we should have known nothing about this trouble, which was very heavy and very great, if she had not left us an account of it. When she was twenty-two years of age she wrote a little autobiography of her own inner life, which you will see was far from being as bright as her outer one. How many a girl, or woman, when she reads, as hundreds of thousands have done, that simple but deeply thoughtful unveiling of a girl's inner life, must have exclaimed with wonder: "Ah! that is just what I am feeling!" or, "So I felt when I was young!"

The great trouble and sorrow of her young life were that she felt she ought to love God, but that she did not. "Up to the time I was six years old," she writes, "I have no remembrance of any religious ideas whatever; I do not think I could ever have said any of those 'pretty things' that little children often do, though there were sweet and beloved and holy ones round me who must have often tried to put good thoughts into my little mind. But from six to eight I recall a different state of things. The beginning of it was a sermon at Hallow. Of this I even now retain a distinct impression. It was to me a very terrible one, dwelling much on hell and judgment, and what a fearful thing it is to fall into the hands of the living God. This sermon haunted me. I began to pray a good deal, though only night and morning, with a sort of fidget and impatience, almost angry at feeling so unhappy, and wanting and expecting a new heart, and to have everything put straight and be made happy all at once.

"This sort of thing went on at intervals, for often a month or two would pass without a serious thought or a true prayer. At such times I utterly abominated being 'talked to,' and would do anything on earth to get away. Any cut or bruise (and such were more the rule than exception in those wild days of tree-climbing, wall-scaling, etc.) was a reason why I could not possibly kneel down when dear M—— offered prayer for me. Then after a time of this sort, some mere trifle, a calm, beautiful evening, or a 'Sunday book' would rouse me up to uncomfortableness again.

One sort of habit I got into in a steady way; every Sunday afternoon I went alone into a little front room over the hall and read a chapter in the Testament, and then knelt down and prayed for a few minutes, after which I usually felt soothed and less naughty. Once when Marian P—— was my only little visitor, I did not like any omissions, and so took her with me, saying a few words of prayer 'out of my head' without any embarrassment at her presence.

"I had a far more vivid sense of the beauty of Nature as a little child than I have even now. I have hardly felt anything so intensely since, in the way of a sort of unbearable enjoyment. The golden quiet of a bright summer's day used to enter into me and do me good. What only some great and rare musical enjoyment is to me now, the shade of a tree under a clear blue sky, with a sunbeam glancing through the boughs, was to me then. But I did not feel happy in my very enjoyment; I wanted *more*. I do not think I was eight when I hit upon Cowper's lines, ending:

'My Father made them all!'

That was what I wanted to be able to say; and, after once seeing the words, I never saw a lovely scene again without being *teased* by them.

"One spring (I think 1845) I kept thinking of them, and a dozen times a day said to myself, 'Oh, if God would but make me a Christian before the summer comes,' because I longed so to enjoy His works as I felt they could be enjoyed.

"All this while I don't think any one could have given the remotest guess of what was passing in my mind. I *knew* I was a 'naughty child'; in fact, I almost enjoyed my naughtiness in a savage, desperate kind of way, despairing of getting better, except by being made a Christian."

In her latest little book, "Kept for the Master's Use," published after her death, she tells us how, at this time, she longed for some one (who did not belong to her own family, to whom she would not listen, good and holy though she knew them to be) to tell her about Christ. She says good men used to come and preach beautiful sermons in her father's church, but when they went home with them they talked of all sorts of other things, "and I did so wish they would talk about the Saviour whom I wanted, but had not found. It would have been so much more interesting to me, and oh! why didn't they ever talk to me about Him, instead of about my lessons or their little girls at home? They did not know how a hungry little soul went empty away."

When she was about nine, Frances left the large Henwick garden, where she had played with her dear dog Flora, for the town rectory of St. Nicholas. Her father called her in those days "a caged lark." "There," she writes, "I had a tiny room of my own; its little window was my 'country,' and soon the sky and the clouds were the same sort of relations to my spirit that trees and flowers had been.

"Soon a sermon by the curate, on 'Fear not, little flock,' struck me very much. I did so want to be happy and a 'Christian.' I had never yet spoken to any mortal about religion; but now I was so uneasy, that after nearly a fortnight's hesitation, being alone with the curate one evening, when almost dark, I told him my trouble, saying I thought I was getting worse. He said moving and coming to new scenes was the cause, most likely, of my feeling worse, and that it would soon go off; I was to try to be a good child and pray, etc., etc. So after that my lips were utterly sealed to all but God for five years."

When Frances was eleven the most terrible sorrow a child can know fell upon her.

After long suffering, her mother died.

The poor child's grief was intense, for she had clung wildly to hope until the very last, and even after her mother had passed away she had still tried to believe that she was but in a trance. "And so," she tells us herself, "when no one was near she had gone again and again into that room and drawn the curtain aside, half expecting to see the dear eyes unclose, and to feel the cold cheek warm again to her kiss."

She has left a touching word-picture of herself, standing by the window in a front room, looking through a little space between the window and blind. All the shops were shut up, though it was not Sunday.

She knew it would be dreadful to look out of that window, and yet she felt she *must* look. She did not cry, she only stood and shivered in the warm air. Very slowly and quietly a funeral passed out of the rectory gate, and in another minute was out of sight turning into the church. Then she stood no longer, but rushed away to her own little room, and flung herself on her little bed, and cried : " Oh, mamma! mamma! mamma!" It seemed as if there were nothing else in her little heart but that one word. All the strange hope of the past week was gone ; she knew that she was motherless.

But though her grief was very deep, she ever tried to conceal it; nor, indeed, was it always heavy upon her, for she had the happy faculty, common to most children (or, poor wee things, how could they live at all through a great sorrow!) of forgetting everything else for the moment when some new interest occupied her attention. "Thus," she writes, " a merry laugh or a sudden light-heeled scamper led others to think I had not many sad thoughts, whereas not a minute before my little heart was heavy and sad."

After her mother's death she was often a good deal with her eldest sister, Miriam, at Oakhampton, where she is remembered as a clever, amusing child, sometimes a little wilful and troublesome from mere excess of animal spirits, but always affectionate and grateful for any little treat ; much given to reading poetry, and not so tidy as she afterwards became, for she used to leave books about in the hay-loft, manger, and all sorts of garden nooks.

But all this while the little girl still carried about with her, wherever she went, that burden of hidden trouble she had borne so long. "I know," the autobiography goes on, "I did not love God; the very thought of Him frightened me." She would try to force herself to think about God, hard as it was to do so. Going to bed, she would begin, "How good it was of God to send Jesus to die," while she by no means felt or believed that wonderful goodness. No one had written "Little Pillows" in those days, nor had rung for children "Morning Bells."

"Between thirteen and fourteen," Frances writes, "a soberising thoughtful time seemed to fall on me like a mantle, and my strivings were no longer the passionate spasmodic meteor flashes they had been, but something deeper, more settled, more sorrowful. All this was secret, and only within my own breast; very few knew me to be anything but a careless, merry girl, light-hearted in the extreme. Now came a more definite and earnest prayer, for *faith*. Oh, to believe in Jesus, to believe that He had pardoned me! I used to lie awake in the long summer twilight praying for this precious gift. I read a great deal of the Bible in a 'straight on' sort of way. Once I determined, if eternal life were in the Scriptures, find it I *would*, and resolved to begin giving an hour a day to very careful and prayerful reading of the New Testament.

"August 15th, 1850, to my great delight, I was sent to school. The night before I went, Ellen, dear, gentle, heavenly sister, stood by me brushing my hair. She spoke of God's love. I could not stand it, and for the first time for five years I spoke out; 'I can't love God yet, Nellie,' was all I said, but I felt a great deal more. Mrs. Teed, the principal of the school, had a sweet and holy power. She prayed and spoke with us with a fervour I have never seen equalled. There were many Christian girls. I envied them. Mary was one. I longed to tell her how unhappy I was. At last I did. The simple, loving words of my little Heaven-taught schoolfellow brought dewy refreshment to my soul as she said, in French (we always had to speak French): Jesus said, 'Suffer the little children,' etc. It is every little child who ought to come to Him, every little child whom He calls, every little child whom He embraces.

"After this I had many talks with Mary, but with no one else. To Diana, the goddess among my school friends, and whom I believed to be like Mary, not a word could I speak; though I longed to hear her speak to me as Mary did.

"I drank in every word I heard about Jesus and His salvation. I came to see that it was Christ *alone* that could satisfy me. I wept and prayed day and night; but 'there was no voice nor any that answered.' I shall never forget the evening of Sunday, December 8th. Diana, whom I loved with a perfectly idolatrous affection, had hardly seen me all day. For some time I had noticed a slight depression about her. That evening, as I sat nearly opposite to her at tea, I could not help seeing (nobody could) a new and remarkable radiance about her countenance. It seemed literally lighted up from within; while her voice, even in the commonest remarks, sounded like a song of gladness. I looked at her almost with awe. As soon as tea was over she came round to my side of the table, sat down by me on the form, threw her arm around me and said: 'Oh Fanny, dearest Fanny, the blessing has come to me at last. Jesus has forgiven me, I know. He is my Saviour, and I am so happy! Only come to Him and He will receive you. Even now He loves you, though you don't know it.'

"Having broken the ice at Belmont (my school), it was the less difficult to do so again; and before long I had a confidante in Miss Cooke, who afterwards became my loved mother. We were visiting at the same time at Oakhampton, and had several conversations, each of which left me more earnest and hopeful. At last, one evening in the twilight, I sat on the drawing-room sofa alone with her. I told her how I longed to know I was forgiven; how even my precious papa, brothers and sisters, all I loved were nothing in comparison. She paused, and then said slowly: 'Then, Fanny, I think, I am *sure* it will not be very long before your desire is granted, your hope fulfilled.' After a few more words, she said : ' Why cannot you trust yourself to your Saviour at once? Supposing now, at this moment, Christ were to come, could you not trust Him? Would not His call, His promise, be enough for you? Could you not commit your soul to him, to your Saviour, Jesus?'

"Then came a flash of hope across me, which made me feel literally breathless. I remember how my heart beat. 'I *could*, surely,' was my response; and I left her suddenly and ran away upstairs to think it out. I flung myself on my knees in my room, and strove to realise the sudden hope. I was very happy at last; I could commit my soul to Jesus. I could trust Him with my all for eternity. It was so utterly new to have any bright thoughts about religion that I could hardly believe that it could be so.

"Then and there I committed my soul to the Saviour; I do not mean to say without *any* trembling or fear, but I did; and earth and heaven seemed bright from that moment; *I did trust the Lord Jesus.*

"For the *first* time my Bible was sweet to me, and the first passage I distinctly remember reading, in a new and glad light, was the fourteenth and following chapters of St. John's Gospel."

This was in February, 1851, when Frances Havergal was fourteen. With this new glad light there came to her a great eagerness for study. She threw herself into her lessons with intense enjoyment until

December came, when a severe attack of erysipelas in her face and head put a stop to the work she loved only too well. She was at once taken home, and was for some time nearly blind.

She bore it with great patience, although it was a great trial to one of her active temperament. She was so extremely agile in every movement, a very fairy with her golden curls and light step, that her father used to call her his "Little Quicksilver." To lie still was a difficult task for her; but to know that she must neither go to school nor study at home for a long time was indeed dreadful news.

Her father's eyesight was now causing his family great anxiety. He had married the Miss Cooke whose words had done Frances so much good; and after Frances had been away from school for some months, and had grown well again in North Wales, she accompanied Mr. and Mrs. Havergal to Germany, where her father placed himself under the care of a great oculist, and his daughter in the Louisenschule, Dusseldorf. Her progress was wonderful there. Here is her own account of the position she took :—

"All the masters were so well pleased with the English girl's papers and conduct that they honoured me with a *Numero* 1, a thing they had never done before. In religion I stood alone (as far as I know) among a hundred and ten girls. This was very bracing. There was very much enmity to any profession, and I came in for more unkindness than would have been possible in an average English school."

Leaving school, Frances spent a little time in the home of a German pastor, where she was very happy. "I get up at five, breakfast at seven; then study for four hours. My books are nearly all German, and I write abstracts. How I do enjoy myself when I get to the German poets and Universal History, which I dive into with avidity!"

After her death, Pastor Schulze-Berge wrote to her sister: "I instructed her in German composition, literature, and history; I learned to appreciate her rich talents and mental powers. She showed from the first such application, such depth of comprehension, that I can only speak of her progress as extraordinary. What imprinted the stamp of nobility upon her whole being was her true piety, and the deep reverence she had for her Lord and Saviour, whose example penetrated her young life through and through."

At home, although supposed to be "finished," she carefully kept up her foreign studies, and by her father's help learned Greek enough to be able to enjoy studying the New Testament.

Her pen was always going. It seemed a sort of tap connected with her brain that could be turned on only too easily. Of course, the young people who would give anything, as they say, to be able to write, wonder and envy this fast-flowing pen. But a flowing pen is a very doubtful literary gift: don't envy it. Write, if you must write, with the pen you have. The tap-like pen often runs mere twaddle or gush, unless it draws its supplies from a well-stocked brain.

Frances Ridley Havergal, at eighteen or nineteen, wrote and wrote and wrote. She would send her enigmas and charades to various "pocket-books" (which in those days used to contain such things), get prizes for them, and give the money to the Church Missionary Society. Her brain was full of "wild, lovely, intangible ideas flitting across her mind, like the shadows of a flying bird," and she was always trying to fly after them.

In her twentieth year she paid her first visit to her sister Ellen (Mrs. Shaw), who was married, and living in Ireland. An Irish schoolgirl thus describes her: "Mrs. Shaw brought us into the drawing-room. In a few seconds Miss Frances, carolling like a bird, flashed into the room! Flashed, yes, like a burst of sunshine, like a hill-side breeze, and stood before us, her fair sunny curls falling round her shoulders, her bright eyes dancing, and her fresh sweet voice ringing through the room. I shall never forget that afternoon, never! I sat perfectly spell-bound as she sang chant and hymn with marvellous sweetness, and then played two or three pieces of Handel, which thrilled me through and through.

"As we girls walked home down the shady avenue, one and another said: 'Oh, isn't she lovely!

and doesn't she sing like a born angel!' 'I love her, I do; and I'd follow her every step of the way back to England if I could.' 'Oh, she's a real Colleen Bawn!' Another felt there must be the music of God's own love in that fair singer's heart; and that so there was joy in her face, joy in her words, joy in her ways. And the secret cry went up from that young Irish heart: 'Lord, teach me, even me, to know and love Thee too.'"

But Frances herself felt very keenly that she was only a little child in the spiritual life. "Gleams and glimpses," she writes in 1858, "but, oh, to be filled with joy and the Holy Ghost! oh, why cannot I trust Him fully?" She read and learned the Scriptures systematically with her friend, Elizabeth Clay (the one to whom she so constantly wrote). In their country walks Frances and her sister Maria would repeat whole chapters in alternate verses. She knew by heart the whole of the New Testament, the Psalms, and Isaiah when about twenty-two, and afterwards learned the minor prophets. Her home life was beautiful, though only one knew the self-restraint and the self-denial of actions, trivial in themselves, but wrought for love to God.

The first definite notice of a literary success outside her own circle is dated 1863, when she was about twenty-seven. She had been asked for poetical contributions by the editor of a monthly magazine, and received a cheque for £10 17s. 6d

This was much more than she had expected. She at once sent it to her father for Church purposes. Her father's note on receiving it was found among her papers: "My dear little Fan can hardly think how much her poor papa loves her, thinks about her, and prays for her. Yes, he does. Thank you, dear child, for remembering me; I will keep all your love, but not the cheque. Our God send you His sweetest and choicest blessings."

Her father died suddenly in 1870, to the intense grief of his family. This loss, however, as all other losses, only made the Divine promises more real to Frances. "Thou art the Helper of the fatherless," flashed brightly upon his daughter soon afterwards when puzzling over a tune her father would have decided at once. "I think," she adds, "that even in music the Lord is my helper now." She now added hymn tunes to her other work.

She had grown much in simple trustfulness. "Writing is praying with me. You know a child would look up at every sentence and say, 'And what shall I say next?' That is just what I do; I ask Him that at every line He would give me not merely thoughts and power, but also every *word*, even the very *rhymes*."

Three years or so after this we, however, find her declaring that she had recently received a blessing that had "lifted her whole life into sunshine, of which all she had previously experienced was but as pale and passing April gleams compared with the fulness of summer glory."

This blessing came to her through a tiny book called "All for Jesus." It set forth a fulness of blessing to which she felt she had not attained. She was gratefully conscious of having for many years loved the Lord, and delighted in His service; but "I want," she wrote, "to come nearer still, to have full realisation of John xiv. 21." A few words on the power of Jesus to *keep* those who abide in Him made her joyously exclaim: "I see it all; I HAVE the blessing!" "I saw it," she says, "as a flash of electric light, and what you *see* you can never *unsee*. There must be full surrender before there can be full blessedness. He Himself showed me all this most clearly."

"One of the intensest moments of my life was when I saw the force of that word 'cleanseth.' The utterly unexpected and altogether unimagined sense of its fulfilment to me, on simply believing in its fulness, was just indescribable. I expected nothing like it short of heaven. Thus accepting, in simple unquestioning faith, God's commands and promises, one seems to be at once brought into intensified views of everything. Never before did sin seem so hateful, watchfulness so necessary, and with a keenness and uninterruptedness, too, beyond what one ever thought of, only somehow different; not a distressed but a happy sort. Then, too, the "*all* for

Jesus" comes in; one sees there is no half-way, it must be absolutely *all* yielded up, because the least unyielded or doubtful point is sin, let alone the great fact of owing all to Him."

Every visit seemed now to open doors for her loving words, and she longed for whole households to taste with her the goodness of the Lord.

About this time she wrote her Consecration Hymn, perhaps the most widely known of all her writings. This is how it came into being. "I went," she writes, "for a little visit of five days. There were ten persons in the house, some unconverted and long prayed for, some converted, but not rejoicing Christians. He gave me the prayer, 'Lord, give me *all* in this house!' And He just *did!* Before I left every one had got a blessing."

"The last night of my visit I was too happy to sleep, and passed most of the night in praise and renewal of my own consecration, and these little couplets formed themselves and chimed in my heart one after another, till they finished with, *Ever*, ONLY, ALL for Thee!"

From December, 1873, the date of reading the little book "All for Jesus," she literally carried out her now famous couplet,

> "Take my voice, and let me sing,
> Always, only, for my King."

She had both a great taste for music and a good knowledge of harmony, a natural and inherited turn for melody, a ringing touch on the piano, a beautiful and well-trained voice. These gifts she now entirely devoted to Christ; whether at home or in mixed society she always "sang for Jesus."

"I was," said she, "at a large regular London party lately, and I was so happy. He seemed to give me the secret of His presence, and, of course, I sang for Jesus, and did I not have a dead silence? Afterwards I had two really important conversations with strangers."

In the early part of 1874 she was expecting to have made a firm literary footing in America, when instead of the £35 due to her, she received the news that her publisher had failed. He held her written promise to publish only with him as the condition of his launching her books, so this seemed quite to close America to her. "Positively," she wrote, "I did not feel it at all, although I had built a good deal on my American prospects; now, 'Thy will be done' is not a sigh but only a *song!*"

That same year (1874), after a happy autumn holiday, she was returning from Switzerland in perfect health, when somehow or another she caught fever. When she reached her home, at Leamington, she was very unwell, and was soon utterly prostrate with typhoid fever. For a while she hovered between life and death. Prayer was continually made for her recovery by a very large number of friends. "Only," she said, when getting better, "I did *not* want them to pray that I might get well at all. I never thought of death as going through the dark valley, or down to the river; it often seemed to me a going up to the golden gates."

Some months later, when threatened with a relapse, she said to her sister Maria, "I felt sure illness was coming on; and, as I lay down, the sweet consciousness that I was just lying down in His dear hand was so stilling."

Her recovery was extremely slow, but her room was the brightest in the house. At last she was carried down stairs, but for some time used crutches. "So delicate with her needle," as many other writing women have been, working for the Zenana Missions was a great pleasure to her during her long convalescence. It was a year before she was able to use her pen except for letters.

When sufficiently well she spent a long while in preparing "Songs of Grace and Glory." "I remember the day it was completed," writes her sister; "she came down from her study with a large roll for post, and with holiday glee exclaimed, 'There, it is all done! Now I am free to write a book!'"

A week after it was burned, stereotype plates and all. The work had to be gone over again. Every chord of her own had to be reproduced; every chord of others re-examined and revised. Frances, however, was able to write of this disaster: "I have thanked

Him for it more than I have prayed about it. He is giving me the opportunity *over again* of doing it more patiently."

The interesting details of the foreign trips she so much enjoyed must all be left out for want of space. When in Switzerland she wrote home a number of descriptive letters and poems, which have been published under the title of "Swiss Letters and Alpine Poems." She was an enthusiastic mountain climber, and once was within a hair's breadth of what must have proved a fatal accident. In a sweet, brave way, she took all the details of her life, whether pleasant or painful, as from the hand of Christ Himself.

When in Switzerland on one of the holiday trips she so much enjoyed, with the full range of the Jungfrau and Silberhorn in view, she caught a chill by getting wet through in a thunderstorm, and was seriously ill for a month, suffering many weary hours of pain.

"One afternoon," writes Maria Havergal, "after trying a new remedy, I begged her to shut her eyes and try to sleep. When I returned she gave me the lines, 'I take this pain, Lord Jesus.' 'You see,' she said, 'I know something of the sweetness of taking pain direct from His hand. I had just been saying all this to the Lord, and then it came to me in this hymn; it wants no correction; I always think God gives me verse when it comes so, and it is worth any suffering if what I write will comfort some one at some time! While I was in such pain, the very lines I've been waiting for came to me. Very often strangers write and tell me that my lines comfort or help them, even when I know there is not a spark of poetry in them. Now *I* cannot tell what will comfort others, so I ask God to let me write what will do so."

This is only one among many incidents that reveal how truly the longings expressed in her "Worker's Prayer" (perhaps the most beautiful of all her hymns) were the truest and deepest utterances of her own soul.

"Lord, speak to me, that I may speak
In living echoes of Thy tone;
As Thou hast sought, so let me seek
Thy erring children, lost and lone."

This sweet and earnest prayer has been so abundantly answered, Miss Havergal's written words have been made so true a blessing to such thousands of souls, that anything like criticism would seem almost sacrilegious; all we can devoutly and thankfully say is, she was one whose work the King, *her King*, manifestly delighted to honour. The King Himself crowned her.

But as well as the hymns, verses, little books, and other sacred work which she was continually producing, she has left behind several books of poems and letters on subjects we may venture to speak of. This large mass of writing would take a great deal more space than we have here to sift and analyse. Like most writers with a swift pen, she wrote far too much ; not indeed for her thousands of devoted readers, who eagerly seek out every scrap she wrote, but for her own permanent literary reputation. These poems and letters, always sweet, pure, and with a singularly bright flash in them, are exceedingly uneven in merit. They easily fall into the three classes of good, bad, and indifferent. But nearly all of them appeal vividly and at once to the average British ear, intelligence, and fancy ; for although she was not a great poetess, she was essentially a singer, and her singing was true and helpful. To her had been committed the Ministry of Song, a ministry not for the literary few, but for the weary many.

In May, 1878, Mrs. Havergal passed away, after long and intense suffering ; to witness which, wrote Frances, has " been by terrible things answering my eager prayer for more teaching and closer drawing at any cost." The home at Leamington was broken up. Frances and Maria set up housekeeping together near the Mumbles, on the Welsh coast. Maria went there first. When Frances joined her, her first words were : " I wanted so to get to you, Maria dear ! " She was so very tired, that even the sea air and perfect rest failed to refresh her for some time. Afterwards she enjoyed scrambles on the cliffs, or getting up to the top of the Mumbles lighthouse, and making the keeper tell her all he knew. Her tastes were very simple. She delighted in wild flowers, and in animals, from the great St. Bernard dogs to her pet kittens.

The sisters arranged a cosy study in their Welsh home; "My work-shop," Frances called it. By the door was her motto, "For Jesus' sake only," and her temperance pledge card. The portrait of her father and other relatives hung near. Then there was her choice little library of books on all sorts of subjects, her desk and writing-table, her favourite chair—a relic of the childish days she spent at Astley Rectory —and the American type-writer she found such a relief to her tired eyes. She was wonderfully neat and methodical in all her arrangements. Her many letters were all carefully docketed; paper and string in their own corners; no litter ever allowed. "'*In order*' (1 Cor. xiv. 40) is something *more* than being *tidy!* Something analogous to 'keeping rank.'"

She contrived a stand for her harp-piano, and there she composed her hymn tunes. Often she turned to the little instrument as a relief from severer work.

Early rising and early studying were her rule; and she was careful to avoid late hours. At seven in the morning during summer, and at eight in winter, she was at her table studying her Bible.

How diligently she studied that Bible the page given in her "Life" will show. Its margin is full of references in the clearest, most minute hand, with carefully ruled lines connecting the thought or idea of one verse to the same thought, or perhaps its contrast, in another.

She was very particular about the cross-readings in her Bible. Sometimes, on bitterly cold mornings, Maria would beg her to read with her feet by the fire. "But then," Frances would reply, "I can't rule my lines neatly; just see what a find I've got! If one only searches, there are such extraordinary things in the Bible!"

She never spared herself. People wrote to her on every conceivable subject, and she was only too ready to answer and help. "What shall I do?" she writes "your letter would take two hours to answer, and I have not two minutes; fifteen to twenty letters to write every morning, proofs to correct, editors waiting for articles, poems and music I cannot touch, American publishers clamouring for poems or *any* manuscripts, four Bible readings or classes weekly, many anxious ones waiting for help, a Mission week coming, and other work after that. And my doctor says my physique is too weak to balance the nerves and brain, and that I ought not to touch a pen." But it was a sad wearing away of her strength. She longed for a lull in her life; but the lull never came. "Dear wearied sister!" Maria adds, "Once she said: 'I do hope the angels will have orders to let me alone a bit, when I first get to heaven!'" Yes, with all her many gifts she had never learned how to conjugate the verb "to laze!" An innumerable host of little things to be done for others continually oppressed her; yet she always wrote pleasantly and cheerily, refreshing others, although she was only too literally wearied to death herself.

A plan of work for 1879 was found in her desk, but before Midsummer came she had been called to her home to the land where work and rest are one.

Many of us remember the little sky-blue book with the golden stars and celestial crown which gave an account of the last week of Frances Ridley Havergal's earthly life, and the cry of mingled grief and triumph that went up from tens of thousands of Christian hearts when it was known that the sweet singer who had been so helpful to them would sing to them no more, on earth, for ever.

On May the 21st, 1879, Frances Havergal returned home wet and chilly. The next day, being Ascension Day, she was so very tired after church, that she rode home on a donkey. Quite a procession of boys followed her, listening eagerly to all she said.

Fred Rosser, her donkey-boy, remembers that she told him: "I had better leave the devil's side; that Jesus Christ's was the winning side, and wouldn't I choose Him for my captain." That was the last time she was out. Four days afterward she corrected the proof of "Morning Stars," and then lay down her pen for ever.

She was not suffering much then, lying quietly in bed, her pet kittens Trot and Dot near her. Then fever and all the agony of peritonitis came on rapidly; but her peace and joy shone through the severest sufferings. When they were distressed for her, she whispered, "It's home the faster!"

"God's will is *delicious;* He makes no mistakes."

Nothing alleviated the agonising pain; but again and again she was heard through the last hours murmuring "So beautiful to go!" The vicar of Swansea came in for a few minutes. He said, "You have talked and written a great deal about the King. Is Jesus with you now?" "Of course!" she answered. "Oh, I want all of you to speak *bright*, BRIGHT words about Jesus! Oh do, do! It is all perfect peace, I am only waiting for Jesus to take me in." Later, whispering the names of many dear ones, she added, "I love them all! I want all to come to me in heaven; tell them to trust Jesus." Then clearly, though faintly, she sang the whole of the verse beginning: "Jesus, I will trust Thee," to her own tune "Hermas." Then came a terrible convulsive sickness. It ceased. The nurse gently assisting her, she nestled down in the pillow, folded her hands, saying, "There, now it is all over! Blessed rest!"

She looked up steadfastly as if she saw the Lord. For ten minutes they watched that almost visible meeting with her King, and her countenance was so glad, as if she were already talking to Him.

Then she tried to sing; but after one sweet high note, "He—," her voice failed, and as her brother commended her soul into her Redeemer's hands, she passed away to meet the King in His beauty.

(*Our Portrait is from a Photograph by Elliott and Fry, London*).

CATHERINE MARSH.

MANY years ago I walked over to Beckenham from Sydenham with a party of young friends for the purpose of hearing Miss Marsh speak at her then famous cottage meetings. Like every one else, we had all been reading the "Memorials of Captain Hedley Vicars," that brave young soldier of Christ and of the Queen who had lived and died so nobly in the deadly trenches before Sebastopol, and who dared to take the open Bible for "his colours." We had also heard a great deal about Miss Marsh and her work among the navvies; so having an opportunity of going to Beckenham, we went.

The memory of that evening is still clear and bright:

"Mid many a day struck calm."

I can still see the Crystal Palace shining on the hills, still see the young forms slowly strolling through the level fields, still feel the grave, religious questioning in the restless young hearts.

Presently we left the fields and turned into the highway that wound through a quaint, rustic village. We paused before the old lych-gate with its broad weather-worn covering, we gazed at the solemn avenue of tall, dark yew-trees that led up to the door of Beckenham Church. How grave, how rural, how quiet it was! Then we went on through the antiquated village until we came to the room where the meeting was to be held. It was the ground floor of an old cottage, and was called a coffee shop.

We were much too early. A neat respectable-looking woman was ironing at a table that occupied the centre of the room. There were no signs of preparation; so we went out again and walked about. In due time we returned. The big table had vanished, the room was full of forms, and a number of navvies were heavily pounding in and flinging themselves on to the forms. We were, however, still early, and found good seats.

Presently two ladies, elegantly dressed in the fashion of that day, came in. There had been a wedding at the Rectory, and the ladies had evidently come to the meeting just as they were. The one was the sister of Hedley Vicars, the other—tall, fair, and of commanding presence—was Miss Marsh herself, who at once began the simple service.

She read the fifth chapter of St. Luke. Her comments upon it must have been very striking, because what I remember so vividly is, not the room at Beckenham and the English navvies, but the Jewish fishermen washing their nets by the lake of Gennesaret, the Saviour coming to them and preaching out of their boat, the Divine command, "Launch out into the deep," the multitude of fishes so great that the net brake, and Simon Peter's "Depart from me, for I am a sinful man, O Lord!"

But when it came to that so human outcry, then I knew I was in Beckenham; for then I felt rather than saw that the great rough heads of the navvies were bowing low, that tears were rolling down their cheeks; then I heard the motherless girl who sat next me crying. Then, like rain upon the thirsty earth, seemed the speaker's earnest pleading: "Oh, shall not we the rather reverse the plea, and cry out of the great need of our own hearts, "Come to me and never leave me, Lord Jesus, for I am a sinner lost and undone without Thee!"

* * * * * *

It so fell out that I never visited Beckenham from that never-to-be-forgotten evening until early in 1885.

Everything was as changed as myself. I went alone. The railway carried me over such of the level fields as yet remain below the hills on which stands the Crystal Palace, and past the gardens of innumerable villa residences.

I alighted at a large station in the centre of a wealthy and populous suburban town, where the only thing I could recognise was the very tall spire of the old church. It was a fine afternoon; many carriages, many pretty girls charmingly dressed, many lovely babies arrayed in spotless creaminesses of lace and cashmere, and reposing in luxurious wheeled bassinets, gave the place a particularly well-to-do aspect. The old churchyard was all but overshadowed by a new Town Hall of the "Queen Anne" pattern, glowing with red brick, next to which was a gorgeous "Board of Works," and an equally grand new bank, which turned the corner of a flourishing row of "Queen Anne" shops dignified by the name of the "Parade."

In the midst of all this modern smartness I found the old lych-gate and the yew-trees still surviving, just as you may see them in the frontispiece of Miss Marsh's little book, "A Light for the Line." But the long rows of navvies in their white, stiff-starched smocks—shown also in that frontispiece—who had come to do the last honours to their comrade, Thomas Ward, were all gone. I went through the gate, and found that grave of his. Alas! so stained with rain drips from the yew-trees is it, and so fast is the stone crumbling, that it was with difficulty I made out the noble words:

"Jesus Christ for every man."

Beckenham had passed into other hands. It made me sad to see this memorial so neglected. The church was open, so I went in; it was full of interest. At the west end of the church you are surprised to find deep and lofty galleries rising one above the other, in a manner shocking to the lover of Gothic architecture, but exceedingly interesting and touching to those whose hearts have been thrilled with the accounts scattered through Miss Marsh's books of hard hearts won to Christ in those pews, in those galleries.

This was the passage from Miss Marsh's "A Light for the Line" that was most strongly in my mind while in Beckenham Church : " So warm was the navvies' affection for Thomas Ward's memory, that on the night following his death there was scarcely a dry eye as I told them his last words: 'Jesus Christ for every man. Blessed, blessed Jesus!' We believed that God had a message for them all, as well as for ourselves, in the death of Thomas Ward, and earnestly desired that not one should lose his share of the blessing."

Accordingly, they were all invited to attend the afternoon service in Beckenham Church, previous to the burial. The aisles and many of the pews were crowded with men dressed in white clothes. They joined earnestly in the responses, and some were affected to tears when, at the close of the third collect for the afternoon service, a hymn was sung which seemed almost a paraphrase of Thomas's last words, and of that world-wide Gospel he had preached from his dying bed :

> "Salvation ! Oh the joyful sound !
> 'Tis music to our ears."

Mr. Chalmers (Miss Marsh's brother-in-law), then Rector of Beckenham, preached a beautiful and impressive sermon on "Devout men carried Stephen to his burial, and made great lamentation over him."

Within the chancel rails is a tablet to the beloved memory of Captain Hedley Vicars, and on the opposite wall to it another to Dr. Marsh, the venerable father of the great and good woman who has made Beckenham a household name wherever the English language is read or spoken.

I left the time-honoured sanctuary, and went into the town in search of the coffee-room in which I had heard Miss Marsh speak and pray. A long shop, full of the newest things in saddlery, had been run out from it; although a few genuine old houses still remained intact among the hundreds of "Tudor," "Jacobean," or "Queen Anne" shops and villas. A large and elegant coffee-tavern, however, showed that temperance work was flourishing.

Quite at the other end of the village—the town I mean—when I had despaired of finding any one who remembered Miss Marsh, I espied, standing outside a cottage, an elderly man, so much stiffened by rheumatism as to need a crutch. I felt he must be an old inhabitant, so I asked him if he remembered Miss Marsh. "Aye! that he did! But she'd been gone a long while." We had a little talk about her, which seemed to please him as much as it did me.

"You should have seen her coming along the line to we," he said warmly, "with the mud and slush over the top of her shoes! But she didn't care for that, not she! I come along with the navvies when they come to make the line. Ah! you should have seen her a walking along up the line! And they were a rough lot too, but they took to her; there's none of 'em as 'ud have hurt her. Not they! They liked her too much!"

This was the impression I took home with me; the tall and dignified figure of that devoted woman going up the half-made line in all weathers, that she might take the message of the Gospel to those homeless working men; going again and again until she won from them the exclamation, "We know you cares for our souls!" until she brought many and many a one to Christ, until she was able to show to all the world that a British navvy could be in very deed and truth a Christian and a gentleman.

* * * * * *

Catherine Marsh is the youngest child of most devoted Christians. Her father was Dr. William Marsh, whose memory is still revered as an earnest evangelical clergyman of singular beauty and purity of life, and of great practical benevolence; her mother was all that the wife of such a man should be, a woman of winning countenance and manners, of refined and cultivated mind, with warm affections, and a sweet, self-sacrificing nature that made her the centre of joy in her home. Best of all, she had in early life entirely devoted herself to her Redeemer's service.

She had heard of William Marsh, and of his youthful consecration, before they met. When they met it was but natural that a strong attachment should spring up between them. It was a holy and blessed love given to them by God, which grew and gathered strength as the years passed on, rooted in their firm purpose that in all things Christ should have the pre-eminence.

William Marsh was a curate when he met Miss Tilson, and as the son and heir of the gallant Colonel Sir Charles Marsh, he was welcomed by her family, and an engagement permitted. But after it had lasted only a few months, Sir Charles suddenly lost his property, and Mrs. Tilson thought it right to break off the engagement.

It was a terrible trial to both the young people, yet so keen a sense of the honour due to parents had they, that for more than three years Maria Tilson not only never exchanged a letter with her lover, but even thought it her duty to deny herself the comfort of hearing from their common friends of William Marsh's welfare; while he, as honourably, never attempted the slightest renewal of the intercourse. For three long years, therefore, they could only meet in spirit "in the sanctuary of the presence of their God."

At length they had their reward. The mother's

heart was so deeply touched by her daughter's submission, that during her last, long illness she freely consented to the marriage. Nor was that all; before she died there came from that mother's lips the sweet testimony that her child's conduct had so convinced her of the reality and power of religion, that she had herself sought and found like precious faith in Christ Jesus. This was indeed worth waiting for.

After her marriage to one whom Mr. Simeon, of Cambridge, describes as "that loveliest and most heavenly-minded of men," her character grew and expanded most beautifully; her faith became more simple, her hope more assured, her charity the steady flame which Divine love kindles, and her confidence in her Saviour more entire.

Charles Kingsley has left us a charming portrait of Dr. Marsh, which will not only show us what manner of man he was, but among what influences his children grew up.

"I recollect him now. A man who had been peculiarly graceful and handsome; tall, delicate-featured, with the air noble of the old *régime;* with a voice and manner full of suavity, even to tenderness, which you felt to be sincere from the earnestness of the voice and the honesty of the eye. Belonging to the old evangelical school, to which all later schools owe their vitality, he seemed to me no bigot, but ready to welcome, or at least patiently to hear, novel thoughts which did not interfere with fundamental truth. He belonged in thought, as well as in manner, to a class of ministers which is growing, alas! more rare among us; he fulfilled rather my notion of what the purest German evangelical of the last century must have been like, those who, with Spener and Franke, re-awakened vital Christianity among a dry and dead generation, given up to the letter of Lutheranism and forgetful of its spirit. In his goodness there was no severity; on the contrary, a gentle benignity, which made his presence always a source of happiness to his relatives and friends."

Dr. Marsh was vicar of the small rural living of Basildon when he married, but not long afterwards he removed to St. Peter's, Colchester, where he resided for fifteen years, and where his ministry was very richly blessed. It was at Colchester that Catherine was born.

The home-life of this family was singularly bright and happy. We get many a glimpse of its cheerful, busy piety in the "Memoir of Dr. Marsh," which his daughter Catherine published, and also in "Home Light," a little volume containing a sketch of Mrs. Marsh and a number of her letters.

The children at a very early age followed the example of their parents. "My dear children," writes Mrs. Marsh from Colchester, "are going on delightfully; they spend all their pocket-money on the poor." Catherine was "the baby." Her mother generally writes of her as "Little C.," and to her as "my tenderly beloved little child," or "my most precious little child."

"Little C. is amusing herself with a pen," is about the earliest notice we have of the future authoress of "Hedley Vicars," and "English Hearts and English Hands." It is certainly characteristic.

Catherine Marsh seems to have taken to her pen when quite young; like three out of the four heroines of this volume, and, indeed, in common with most clever girls and boys, she had a trick of writing verses—vigorous verses too.

Here are a few lines which were written inside the cover of her French exercise-book when scarcely more than a child. They give a good idea of the happiness of her young days.

> "Happy my infancy was and gay,
> Sunny and bright as mornings in May;
> When my sweet sisters and brothers played
> With 'the baby' in the chestnut shade,
> Or sauntered in summer in the woods,
> Lighting our fire, and bringing our goods
> For the wondrous charms of a gipsy tea,
> By spreading oak and sycamore tree."

But the children, even "the baby," grew up, and not long after they had again moved, this time to the crowded town of Birmingham, a heavy blow fell upon them. The dear mother was taken.

"Sweet mother!" Catherine Marsh goes on in the little poem just quoted from her "Memory's Pictures"—

> "Sweet mother! all these are fled, and we
> Have lost our childhood in losing thee."

That loss created indeed what Dr. Marsh called a "tremendous vacuum;" he adds, however, "my beloved children do all in their power to comfort me, and try to conceal their own anguish."

The whole family was remarkable for very strong affection, and although the elder branches married and left the old home, their love for it and for the father who was its glory never diminished. Catherine, the youngest, however, devoted herself to her father with all the strength of her loving nature. Both in her memoir of him and in her little verses her father is shown to the world as the centre of her earthly life, her guide and companion to the better land.

About seven years after his wife's death he suffered severely from cataract, and for a time quite lost his sight. Catherine was a most tender nurse to him during that time. For many nights he could only obtain even the short relief of an hour's sleep by listening to the reading of the Bible in a low voice. The New Testament was read through from beginning to end.

"What can we do now our book is finished?" his daughter asked. To which he replied with characteristic playfulness: "Send for a second volume." She relates how

> "He said one weary day
> When he was faint and blind,
> 'Thy gentle arm shall be my stay,
> And there my rest I'll find.'"

And how her very heart was choked with tears, and that she felt that if before her there lay the choice of a long, bright life, or the soothing of his blindness and pain:

> "With all their sadness, I would rather
> Have these still hours with thee, my father."

Happily she was spared the painful choice, for an operation he underwent was successful, and sight was restored.

But Catherine Marsh is so distinctly to the public Miss Marsh of Beckenham, that we must not linger to trace her useful, busy early life as a clergyman's daughter at Birmingham and then at Leamington.

When 1851 arrived Dr. Marsh had already long passed his three-score years and ten, and his charge at Leamington had become too much for him.

His son-in-law, the Rev. F. Chalmers, who had just been presented to the living of Beckenham, begged Dr. Marsh, most affectionately, to come to Beckenham and make a home in its Rectory. He did so, and of course Miss Marsh went with him. They were welcomed with the greatest rejoicing, and at once joined in the rector's many schemes for the good of the neighbourhood with their accustomed energy; but it is not until the summer of 1853 that Miss Marsh seems, in the eyes of the general religious public, to stand out in all her striking individuality.

It is in "English Hearts and English Hands" that Miss Marsh of Beckenham lives and will live for many a year to come. Here, quite unconsciously, in recording what she felt to be God's work, she has drawn her own portrait to the life, while in her father's memoir she has most conscientiously hidden herself; although even when she was quite young the true incidents related in her little books, "The Golden Chain" and "The Rift in the Cloud," which we dare not stay to describe, show the power she has always possessed of knowing how to meet the difficulties of very various minds. Another beautiful instance of this occurred when she was still in her teens, and is told in "Dreamlight from Heaven."

If genuine human feeling can be put into a book, that feeling can never grow old. The author dies, the book itself is pushed aside and buried under huge heaps of new publications, but unearth it, and there you will find the emotion still alive, still throbbing as vigorously as when it was first put on paper.

All Miss Marsh's books are instinct with genuine feeling; but few records in our language are fuller of this strong vitality than her "English Hearts and English Hands." Happily we have not to unearth it, for it has never ceased to be popular; its thirty years have not dimmed its brightness; it is still one of the most living books of its class.

The crowd of rough navvies with their tumultuous joys and sorrows, their struggles for goodness, their sudden falls, all surging round the grand woman who alone could control them, who alone could love and admire them, and draw out their best qualities, live in these wonderful pages; we cannot say they live over again, for they have never ceased to pulsate with strong and genuine emotion.

It was early in 1853 that nearly three thousand navvies invaded the quiet woods on the Sydenham hills for the purpose of turning them into the great pleasure gardens of the Crystal Palace. The villages around soon swarmed with excavators; two hundred went over to Beckenham to lodge, and most of the good people of the neighbourhood began to fear that they would prove very troublesome lodgers. Probably Catherine Marsh may have thought so too, but whatever her forebodings, she at once determined to gain the friendship of these rough new-comers if it were possible to do so.

In those days no one had discovered the navvy's good qualities: with his heavy boots clogged with clay, his earth-coloured clothes and his habit of going about in gangs, the stranger navvy was a person few people cared to have much to do with before Miss Marsh showed the way to his heart.

The two hundred navvies had not been long at

Beckenham before Miss Marsh went out one spring Sunday evening about seven o'clock on her first voyage of discovery.

Several of the men were lodging in a cottage belonging to a family she had formerly visited during the illness of one of its members; so she went, not without trembling doubtless, and asked after her late patient.

A tall strong man in a fustian jacket, who had opened the door scarcely wide enough to allow his face to be seen, replied gruffly, "Harry ain't here just now."

"But I suppose I shall see him if I wait? I will walk in, if you will allow me," said Miss Marsh.

"Well, you can if you like, but we're a lot of rough uns."

Undeterred by the surly response, she went in, saying as she entered, "Would you get me a chair?"

An intelligent-looking young fellow flew forward, dusted a chair with the tail of another man's coat and placed it near the table. Miss Marsh asked them if they had been to church. They said they had never thought of it. So she told them how the morning's sermon had been about a brave, good doctor who had recently died.

Some of the men had known him and had been helped by him. When the little story was ended the young man who had dusted the chair with another man's coat said, "Well, ma'am, it's a beautiful story, but in a measure it passes by me, because I don't believe the Bible. I read in the Bible that God is a God of love, and yet that He has prepared for all eternity a place of torment for us poor, pitiful creatures."

"In *my* Bible," Miss Marsh replied, "I have never read anything of the sort;" and then she went on to show them that in spite of their hard thoughts, it was still eternally true that God *is* Love.

She spoke earnestly for some time, telling them that God so loved the World that He gave His Son, all for one purpose, "to seek and save that which is lost. He is drawing nigh, He is come to you now," she ended; "He is speaking these words of His own by my feeble lips. Are you willing to let Him save you?"

"I am, I am," the young man said with fervour, drawing his chair nearer hers. "I never thought of Him before but as an angry God; you make Him out a *Friend*."

"Shall I pray with you?" asked Miss Marsh.

"I should like it. But *this* man," pointing to one behind him, "never opens his mouth but to swear."

"But he will open it to *pray* now. Will you not, my friend?"

"Yes."

And as they all knelt together, their voices

followed hers, and two or three sobs burst from those strong men.

From this beginning sprang up those wonderful Cottage Bible Readings the story of which has delighted so many thousands of people throughout the world, and set so many of them working for the good of their neighbours.

"English Hearts and English Hands" has proved a most inspiring book; it has been the pioneer of innumerable efforts to reach the working classes. Many are the well-known workers whom Miss Marsh's steady faith and loving resolute perseverance that refuses to be discouraged, have been the means of raising up.

She believed in the Gospel. She believed too that it was the very Christ of that Gospel that her Beckenham navvies needed. According to her faith so it was to her.

Her portraits of the navvies are drawn with a most vigorous but a most loving touch. Here, for instance is "John H——. His fair face, straight features, and almost white hair, were eminently Saxon, and he himself the wildest piece of nature I had then seen." He doesn't go to church, won't hear of such a thing. But she gets him to take a little Testament, and soon we see him sitting down on the doorstep twirling it round between his finger and thumb, and exclaiming, "Now, ain't it a rare beauty? I'll cover it with a slice off my best red choker!"

Miss Marsh had all sorts of womanly ways for getting at these rough fellows. When she was going away from home she wrote notes in large printing characters to them, asking them to attend church regularly, and the next Sunday morning the middle aisle was full of clean stiff white smocks. She asked John H—— if he had received her letter? "A letter, a letter for me!" shouted the laddie with the lint-white locks; "all the way from where you went! Well, the postman did bring me one, and I said ''Tain't for me. Nobody cares to write to me; so I sent it back. But I'll go and pull the post-office about their ears if they don't give it me back again!'"

Very stirring are some of the scenes in that record. Navvies, even under her influence, were sometimes but navvies still. Angry words and furious blows followed too often upon the most generous kindness. Paget, one of her most hopeful men, told her on an evening that was both Sunday and New Year's Day that if "Long George" came to the meeting he should order him out. The whole scene is graphically described, but too long for our space. Miss Marsh pleaded first with one and then went to the other, and separately each one could not let her "go home sorry;" but when after much difficulty she brought them face to face for the purpose of making it up, there came such loud talking that she feared a fight would ensue. Fists were raised and shaken in each other's faces, the men were growing more and more furious, and their threats louder and louder, when Miss Marsh glided in between the two navvies with:

"Oh, Paget! oh, George! We must have no more. Let us kneel down and pray that the God of peace would prove Himself stronger than the devil. At first," she says, "I knelt alone, but soon heard the two men suddenly fall on their knees; and when we rose up the tears were rolling down Paget's cheeks."

"After that prayer," he cried, "I'll forgive him from my heart out."

But still George would not yield. Miss Marsh pleaded desperately with him. He stood irresolute, but sullen.

"Give *me* your hand," she said at last.

"That I will."

"And now, Paget, give me yours." And the two huge, rough hands met in hers.

The whole book is so teeming with living interest that it is hard to leave any of it unnoticed; happily the book itself is very cheap. But in case some one who reads this may not have seen Miss Marsh's description of the battle of Penge, I must condense it here.

The navvies who had been chosen for the Army Works Corps were massed at the Crystal Palace before they were sent out to the Crimean War. Six or seven hundred of these men with their wages in their pockets were kept waiting in idleness there for several days.

Rather fewer than a hundred of these men, who were lodging at Penge, spent a night, which they had every reason to believe would be their last in England, in a drunken revel.

The next afternoon Miss Marsh and her sister drove to the Crystal Palace gates to enquire when the embarkation was likely to take place. Two of the men of business of the corps hurried to the carriage.

"Pray drive down to Penge at once," they said. "There's a fight going on between the police and some of our men, but if you ask them they will go away quietly, drunk or sober." The ladies drove to Penge, where they saw two policemen who had been terribly hurt, and seven men who had been taken prisoners. About fifty navvies, all more or less intoxicated, had formed a ring and had begun boxing. The police had interfered, laying about them with their staves. The mob had been roused to fury, there had been a fight. At the moment of the ladies' arrival the mob had, however, dispersed; but a few minutes later a great crowd of navvies poured down the hill and from the Crystal Palace gates shouting,

"Down with the police! Rescue the prisoners! Punish the police well!"

The police stood their ground steadily, but were soon overwhelmed by the yelling crowd. The moment was come. The ladies drove between the infuriated men, and like Nehemiah, Miss Marsh " prayed to the God of heaven." Then, turning to the crowd of five hundred furious navvies, many of whom had already upraised missiles, she said,

"The first man who throws a stone is my enemy. Go back, and give over, for my sake, for the sake of that God of peace of whom I have so loved to speak with you." There was a brief silence.

"Do you go away, ma'am," then some of them said. "We wouldn't hurt you for anything ; but it is not fair to hinder us paying off the pleece."

"I shall not go away till you are gone, if I stay here till midnight," returned Miss Marsh firmly.

"We don't want to vex you," said two or three spokesmen, " but we *will* set our mates free."

"They *shall* be free," exclaimed Miss Marsh, who, with the navvies, thought "the mates" unjustly made prisoners. "If there's justice in England, they shall be free to go with you to the Crimea. I pledge myself not to rest till it is done. Will you trust me?"

There was a pause, and then a short conference between the leaders was followed by loud shouts of, "Trust ye to the world's end."

"Then prove it by going back within the Crystal Palace gates."

In five minutes Miss Marsh was left alone with the police and the prisoners.

The whole of Miss Marsh's treatment of her

navvies showed equal resolution. One hardly knows which to admire the more, her determination or her tenderness. How beautifully both are united in the following:

One of her most hopeful men having been accused by his mates of being stingy, the one charge the navvy dreads above everything, had, to prove the falseness of the accusation, treated his mates and cleared himself, although he had been obliged to sell his clothes to do so.

When he came to his sober senses again he was terribly distressed. Miss Marsh went to see him. He would not meet her. His wife tried to persuade him to come down, but he said,

"Where's the good of being pulled up to be better for a day or too, only to go down the lower afterwards?"

"Tell him," said Miss Marsh, "that I shall stay here until he comes."

He was a long while coming, but at last he came with slow, unwilling step.

"It is no use at all; I've sold my soul to the devil," he said sullenly.

"But he shall *not* have it; it is not yours to sell. Jesus Christ has bought it with His own blood. Oh, William, I must, I will have it for Jesus Christ!"

She could say no more, her voice failed; but the strong man bowed his head on the table and wept like a child.

But time, or at least my very limited space, would fail to tell of all the good work done at Beckenham, not only by Miss Marsh, but by the whole of the large rectory circle, all of whom seemed to lay out themselves and their belongings entirely for the good of their fellow-creatures, among whom the cadets at Addiscombe College were not forgotten.

Many an officer now growing grey remembers with affection the happy Sundays on the lawn of Beckenham Rectory, when the youngsters gathered around the venerable Dr. Marsh, listening with rapt interest to his words.

"What is the good of being young," said one of the cadets, as he lingered for another smile and parting word, "when one sees a man of eighty in better spirits than the jolliest of us?"

Miss Marsh always took these young soldiers under her especial care. As I write I have before me a copy of "Hedley Vicars," yellow, and stained with twenty years of India, in which is the name of one of those young officers to whom it was given "with Catherine Marsh's kind regards and best wishes."

In 1860 Dr. Marsh was induced, by many considerations, to accept the living of Beddington, Surrey. His daughter continued there a somewhat similar work to that carried on at Beckenham, only instead of navvies there were, beside the villagers, tanners and workers at the leather, snuff, and paper mills that had grown up on the banks of the pretty river Wandle.

Miss Marsh's meeting in the tannery presented a remarkably picturesque scene, and these services too were made channels of great blessing to very many.

In busy work and in devotedly tending the declining age of her most fondly loved father, Catherine Marsh spent four happy years at Beddington, and then the inevitable end came.

On the last night of the long watching, his daughter Catherine printed in large letters to catch his failing sight, the words, "A pillow for my heart's beloved." "God is love." (He says) "I have loved thee with an everlasting love." A few hours after, when the window had been thrown open and the sunshine was streaming in, with serene dignity he raised his hand and closed his own eyes, to draw the curtain that would hide earth from his sight, and leave him alone with his Saviour.

Very deeply did Miss Marsh feel the loss of that father from whom she had never before been parted; and in accordance with his wish that all his letters and papers should be hers, she now occupied herself in writing his life, "a task," as she says in the preface, "at once most painful and most precious." Whilst she was thus occupied, not long after Dr. Marsh was called hence, a dreadful visitation of cholera swept over the east of London, and her heart, ever ready to respond to the cry of the needy and the suffering, impelled her to seek for and to obtain admission to the wards for cholera patients.

These were opened in the London Hospital, Whitechapel Road, where, for the greater part of each day, during the four months' prevalence of cholera, Miss Marsh ministered by the bed-sides of the sick and dying. She has related some of her experiences at this time in a little book called "Death and Life; or, Cholera Wards and Convalescent Homes," from which I give the following touching incident, as it illustrates so forcibly her simple and absolute faith that God will answer prayer, as well as her intense human sympathy with suffering.

After a graphic description of the wards, and of the cholera-stricken patients, and the devotion of the chaplain, the doctors, the nurses, and other helpers, she goes on:

"A young man, named William N——, was suffering very severely, though he firmly suppressed all sign of it, his rapidly changing colour alone betraying it. 'You are in great pain, I fear.'

"'Pain!' he said; 'it *is* pain!'

"The next day the glowing face was reduced to a worn and ashy paleness. By his side stood a young brother, weeping bitterly. The nurse wisely remonstrated with him:

"'You won't give your poor brother a chance if you take on so.'

"'Oh, he'll die! he'll die!' sobbed the lad; 'there is no chance for him.'

"'You're right,' I said, 'there is no "chance" for him; he is in the hand of Almighty God. But the Son of God has said, "If two of you shall agree touching anything on earth, it shall be done unto you of my Father which is in Heaven."'"

"'I never heard those words before. Do you think He would keep to them, now?'

"'Yes, I am sure He would be as good as His word; and will raise your brother up again if He can see it to be best for him. Come, then; if you will be one of those "two," I will be the other.'

"'No! would ye?' and the young face brightened through its tears.

"So we pleaded it together, as we stood side by side.

"The next day William had a faint colour in his cheeks again. The nurse said he had called for some beef-tea soon after I had left, saying, 'We must give the lady's prayers all the chance we can, nurse, or it won't be fair upon her.' She noticed that he 'took heart again from that moment.'

"On the following Monday he met me in the entrance-hall of the Hospital, accompanied by his wife and that young brother, in great joy and thankfulness for his spared life. Shaking my hand heartily, he said, 'We shall never doubt now about God being as good as His word.'"

Only those who have heard Miss Marsh speak and pray can fully understand the helpful power of her presence among such scenes of agony. Her work among the sufferers was, however, not confined to the sick and dying. As soon as patients began to recover she felt very strongly the need of getting them away from the terrible hospital, either to the fresh country or to the sea-side.

An unasked for hundred pounds was sent to her for the benefit of the convalescents, and in three days Miss Marsh had a block of country cottages furnished and ready for their inmates' use. Great, indeed, was the joy of the poor patients, as, amid the shouts of a large crowd of sympathising friends, they were driven off in an open van to the Essex cottages, "instead of," as they said themselves, "going in the dead cart to the cemetery."

The cottages were so great a success, and the sufferers recovered so quickly, that Miss Marsh determined to make a Convalescent Home for them at Blackrock, Brighton. Happily, the cholera disappeared, but Blackrock Home still continues to receive patients from the poor districts of London.

Some thousands of sufferers have enjoyed that hospital home, and in the great majority of cases recoveries have been both rapid and complete. The sea, which many of them had never before seen, made a deep impression on some of the patients. The most thoughtful care provides not only for the actual wants but for the pleasure of the inmates. And when, as has occasionally happened, patients have been sent there too far gone for cure, all that could be done to soothe their last hours has been provided. A wife or mother, a husband or child, has been welcomed, free of expense, to help in nursing and watching the sufferer, and the dying eyes have been, in most cases, led, by the blessing of God, to rest upon a living Saviour ; and in the peace of God which passeth all understanding, one after another has fallen asleep.

Another important work arose out of the cholera epidemic. Many of the poor dying creatures in the London Hospital were terribly anxious about their children, whom they were leaving without protection. The thought of their children's fate was too often the bitterest part of their most bitter pain. How could it be otherwise? How could they

"See their orphans, and not dread the grave?"

"Who is to take care of my children?" they cried. And Miss Marsh could not help answering, "I will; I'll take care of them."

In this way seventy-seven forlorn little beings were committed to her care.

Her sister, Mrs. Chalmers, at once arranged an orphanage at Beckenham for them, in a roomy, old-fashioned house, supplemented by an iron room.

The orphans were brought up as much as possible

on the family system. The boys and girls were taught to help each other, the boys doing such things as cleaning the girls' boots, and the girls mending the boys' socks and clothes. "The sunshiny happiness of their daily life in the Home," writes Miss Marsh six years after its establishment, "has even surpassed our hopes."

But "sunshiny happiness" is one of Miss Marsh's peculiarities, added to which she has the gift of infusing a good deal of the same sort of happiness into others.

When Mr. Chalmers left Beckenham for Nonington, the orphanage was removed there. By that time several of the children had been placed out in service; and as it was not intended to add to the number, the iron house, which had been only a part of the Beckenham establishment, was large enough, and this was re-erected in the grounds of Nonington Rectory until by degrees all the orphans were provided for.

* * * * *

Little did I think when I began this sketch that I was again to have the privilege of hearing Miss Marsh speak; but so it has been ordered.

More than this, I have even seen her the centre of love and reverence in a sweet home where the sacred teaching of the Bible and of the Divine Master penetrates each simple action of daily life through and through.

Since her father's death, Miss Marsh has lived with

one of her nieces, the wife of a clergyman now the rector of a Norfolk parish. When I saw her she had just returned from London, where she had been saying farewell and giving Testaments to many hundreds of our soldiers who were leaving for Egypt, the youth of some of whom had quite gone to her heart.

On Easter Monday, 1885, a large tea party was given by her to about two hundred farm labourers, and here I again heard Miss Marsh address an audience. Years had told in some measure even on her, but her heart seemed as young as ever; she was still as striking an individuality as in the old navvy day. Rows and rows of weather-beaten faces turned to her as if spellbound as to them also she told in that way that is so quite her own, how "God so loved the world."

A story of a navvy's happy death I will try to give you; but it is quite impossible to describe the graphic power of Miss Marsh's own narrative.

"Many years after I had left Beckenham," she said, "I returned one day for a visit. As soon as I reached the rectory door my sister said to me: 'One of your old navvies is dying of consumption, and wants to see you.' I went off at once. When I entered the room I exclaimed:

"'Oh, James Green, how pleased I am to see you again! But so sorry to find you so ill.'

"'There,' cried the man, 'there! I knew you'd know my name! I said you would!'

"'Of course! I remember all about you;' and so I did, for this was the man who had walked forty miles to Beckenham, when he heard that he had been prayed for by name; and when he heard, from the corner where he had concealed himself, that it was perfectly true, his heart seemed melted with gratitude.

"In a few minutes I found that James was not happy. 'I can't understand it, and I can't see how God lets this be; here am I, a skilled workman, and getting on well and making my wife happy, struck down for death, while there's a lot of old people in workhouses, and such-like, no comfort to themselves and a burden to others, that go living on, whilst here's an end of all my happiness; can *that* be right?'

"'But, James,' I said, 'is it an end of all your happiness?'

"'Well,' he replied rather sadly, 'it might be different if I was quite sure I was going to heaven; but I am not. Though I am not a bad fellow like some, but now and again I have taken a drop too much, and *I know* that's sin; and I haven't gone to church regular, or kept Sunday as I should, and *I know* that's sin.'

"I spoke of Christ's death for us, and read 1 John i.: 'If we confess our sins, He is faithful and just to forgive us our sins,' when he stopped me short by saying,

"'That'll do.'

"Thinking he felt tired, I only said, 'Then goodbye, James; I will come again as soon as I can,' and left him. The next day was Sunday, and as I could not walk so far, a young friend, an Addiscombe cadet, went to enquire for James for me. He brought word that James wanted me to go as soon as possible on Monday, adding that he said he 'had a secret that I must hear before any one else; but,' put in my friend, 'it is a very open secret, for it is flashing all over his face.'

"And so it was; his worn features were shining with joy when I saw him the next morning. 'I told you that would do,' was his greeting, '*and it did.*'

"'Oh, James, I thought you meant I had read enough.'

"'Now, did you?' said he; 'no, no, I meant this: if God is *faithful* to forgive us our sins, that's a great thing; but *just*, that's more wonderful still, and means He'll do it at once; for no honourable *man* even would delay to do a justice, how much more God! Then I thought, how is it that He is just to forgive me my sins? and I remembered you told me that Christ had paid the price, so it wouldn't be just to want it paid twice over. So now I am quite happy, and not afraid to die.'

"After that he used to tell all who came to see him of the way to have their sins forgiven. Then his dying night came, and his wife and sister were watching beside him, when he exclaimed,

"'What's that beautiful light in the corner? Why, there's mother in it—dear mother, who died blessing

G

me when I was but seven year old. Dear mother, how pretty she looks! Yes, I'll come to you, mother;' then after a moment's pause, 'I don't see mother's light now, but there's another more beautiful, and I see a face; it's as innocent as a babe's, and yet it's like God. Why, it's the Lord Jesus. Oh, blessed Saviour, how kind to come for me! Yes, I'm ready to go with you,' and leaning back on his pillow he went away."

This narrative gives a good idea of the manner in which Miss Marsh can use a text of Scripture; but no written words can possibly convey to those who have not heard her speak what a text—a well-known text that has become to us, perhaps, like a much used coin, with the impression on it all but worn smooth—can become. The Divine image and superscription grow firm and clear once more, and the pure gold shines as if "fire new from the mint" of the Word of God.

It is not only when addressing an eager and crowded audience that she shows this gift in handling the Word of Life, but always; a text from her lips, whenever heard, is a power indeed.

Is not this a power which even ordinary Christians may cultivate in themselves, and which would doubtless be the possession of many if only they had the same absolute faith in the words they utter?

Long may Miss Marsh be spared to make the Divine Message so clear and plain.

(*Our Portrait is from a Photograph by Elliott and Fry, London.*)

MRS. RANYARD ("L. N. R.").

BETWEEN the gardens of the Thames Embankment and the Strand there stands, raised on arches, a tall row of fine houses well known to Londoners as Adelphi Terrace. From this terrace there is a view unique in all the world. Let us enter No. 2, the Mother House or Centre of the London Bible and Domestic Female Mission, and go upstairs to one of the top rooms, just opposite Cleopatra's Needle, and there look out of an open window.

We will suppose it is a fine clear day in summer. Below us, beyond the garden, is the great crowded Thames, stretching in a noble bend from Lambeth Palace to where far down stream it is lost to sight near Cannon Street Bridge. How full of life it is! There is a fascination about the scene that rivets one to the window! There to the right is the huge railway bridge and station of Charing Cross, with its many trains and its white sun-lighted vapour. Then there are the towers of Westminster beyond; the great sweep of river and gardens and Surrey shore; the Temple, St. Paul's, the aggressive roof of Cannon Street Station, the City, the bridges; the swift steam-boats darting by the slow barges, the never-ceasing play of rippling water, the constant traffic on the broad Embankment; far off on the distant hills is the dim outline of the Crystal Palace; and in the extreme east the turrets of the Tower. One might spend an hour there, and not be weary of that marvellous scene.

But we must leave the window, and just glance through the house. Is it Friday? Then there are Bible-women coming and going. Is it Tuesday? Then the stairs and large upper room are filled with Bible-nurses bringing in their empty bags and taking out others full of medical stores for the poor people among whom they work.

Here there is a cupboard full of Bibles or parts of Bibles. Portions at one penny, and Family Bibles running as high as thirty shillings, all to be paid for a penny at a time. Look at that large-print two-shilling Bible, the greatest favourite of all—the Bible-woman will have to call twenty-four times at the buyer's house before it is all paid for. Let us hope that by that time buyer and seller will be fast friends. In the year 1884 the Bible-women sold nearly twelve thousand Bibles or parts of Bibles, and all were paid for in pennies. Find the value one single text may be to one single soul, multiply by all the texts in the Bible, then multiply the Bible by twelve thousand, add to this the personal influence of an earnest Christian woman, and when you have finished this sum you may be able to arrive at some faint idea of the value of the Bible-women's work.

Near this Bible-cupboard is a store-room, in which an enthusiastic housekeeper would positively revel. There are presses full of endless packages of oatmeal, sugar, cereal food, lint, cotton-wool, lotions, oil-silk, and the tins in which the nurses carry the cooked food. On the mantelpiece is the neatest possible little machine for rolling bandages. There are presses full of garments, new and old, of all sorts and sizes, numberless little new bundles waiting for numberless little new babies, men's suits, women's clothes, children's clothes. Nurses and Bible-women are always taking them out to those who need them so dreadfully, and kind people are always sending others in.

Downstairs in the large council-room a few ladies are managing the affairs of the Mission. You see they form a little group around one lady who is reading reports aloud to them. On the wall above the reader's chair hangs the portrait of the foundress, the late Mrs. Ranyard, and the kindly, penetrating eyes of that motherly face still look down lovingly on those who are carrying on the good work she began.

Invisible persons like ourselves may gaze at that picture without disturbing any one.

The portrait was taken late in Mrs. Ranyard's life, but it is exceedingly characteristic. She was extremely kind and extremely firm. You see both qualities in the keen, deep-set eyes, that seem to judge and weigh and penetrate, but never pierce; in the shrewd, almost humorous expression of the mouth; in the pleasant smile. How beloved that face was in life, and how tenderly regretted now! Those who worked with her can scarcely yet say calmly, "I can't tell you what she was like, but I have her in my heart! Oh, she was kind—kind—kind! She was unique, there was never any one like her!"

These are the sort of answers, spoken with tears welling up in the eyes, that tell more than words how much she is missed, when one tries to find out what manner of woman Mrs. Ranyard was.

* * * * *

Ellen Henrietta White—this was Mrs. Ranyard's maiden name—was born at Nine Elms in 1809, and was the eldest of a large family of brothers and sisters. In those days Nine Elms was a comparatively quiet river-side place. Now it is entirely occupied by a gigantic goods-station. Ellen White's parents were both of them most excellent people, but very dissimilar in character. The father was an exceptionally kind and gentle man, the mother kind also, but a most rigid maintainer of discipline. Both were very energetic in their different ways, and their many children took after both of them.

Mr. White was a prosperous business man, and he and his wife looked well to the education of their children, giving them such culture as was then to be had, but training them with especial care in the knowledge of the Scriptures and of the "Shorter Catechism."

In such an atmosphere Ellen White early developed a taste for books and art, and a passionate longing for bringing out the best of what she felt was in her. Her brothers and sisters still remember her as "the good elder sister," and "good" not only in the way of kindness, although she was always their comforter in their troubles, but as their inspirer, their helper in their strivings after knowledge, and in the development of their mental and spiritual powers.

Beyond, however, this vague striving after self-improvement, Ellen White does not appear to have arrived at any definite idea of giving herself up to any particular form of usefulness. When she was sixteen or thereabout, in 1826, the future of her coming life had thrown no shadow upon her. Then one of those epoch-making events that mark the beginning of a new era in the chronology of a life took place.

She has left but few notes of her history behind her, but this event she has recorded at some length. It shall be given in her own words. It is headed :—

THE BEGINNING OF MY LIFE-WORK.

"My mission history begins when, as a girl of sixteen, I was taken by my parents to a Bible-meeting at Wanstead. We were to stay with the family who entertained the speakers, in which there were several daughters, one of whom, Elizabeth Saunders, was at this time about to part with a dear friend, to whom she owed her conversion. They had been next-door neighbours, and when this dear friend had left for Manchester, Elizabeth, a gentle and loving soul, felt that she should stand alone in her family, who were at that time unconverted. Her heart seemed half-broken, and I remember that an elder friend tried to comfort her with these lines :

> God nothing does, nor suffers to be done,
> But thou wouldst do thyself if thou couldst see
> The end of all things here as well as He.'

"I felt much for their sorrow, and so did my mother, and she entreated Mrs. Saunders to let Elizabeth return home with us for a little change. The two friends had been the 'evangelists' of their village, and the one left behind was in delicate health and low spirits. Her parents thought she had exerted herself too much, and it was understood that she was to come to us for rest. There was, however, no rest for her but in bringing souls to Jesus.

"One morning I sat at a table drawing [until her life's end Ellen White never lost her love for drawing and painting; but art schools where girls could study were unknown in those pre-South

Kensingtonian times, so the poor things had to do the best they could without them, and that best was not very much after all]; we were alone, and Elizabeth said to me:

"'Ellen, dear, have you ever thought what you will do with your life?'

"'Do with my life?' I answered; 'well, I hope I shall go on cultivating my mind and my faculties; that is all I have thought about yet.'

"'Yes; but have you thought that this cultivation is to enable you the better to live for others, not for yourself, and that you must live to do something in God's service?'

"'Perhaps you mean in a Sunday school? My mother will not let me teach there. She says such work is only for converted people, and I am not converted. I like worldly reading, such as the *Literary Gazette*, and Lord Byron's poetry [Byron was then the idol of nearly everybody, and especially of all the *young* bodies and minds], and I wish to see more of the world before I leave it, especially of its books.'

"'Then you mean to leave it some time? I wonder what, my dear, you know about the Best of Books? do you love your Bible at all?'

"'I have read it through three times; I seem to know all about it. Yes, certainly I love it; but one cannot always be reading one's Bible.'

"'I suppose you never have thought how many

of the poor people who live in the streets not far from you have no Bible to read?'

"I answered, 'No, I never thought of that, but I liked your Bible meeting very much the other day at Wanstead.'

"'Would you like to leave your painting this morning, and go with me to find out how many want a Bible?'

"'Yes, I should like to go anywhere with you, but it would be like Sunday-school, and I suppose my mother would not approve; and she may also say that you came here to rest yourself from all you do at home.'

"This dear Elizabeth, however, had set her heart on the exploring walk, and she obtained my mother's consent under protest, I remember, for she looked anything but fit for the exertion, and was made to take egg and wine as a fortifier before going out. So we set forth, she with a Bible in her hand and a prayer in her heart, and in her pocket a pencil and a little book, a page or two of which she had been ruling in squares while I had been painting by her side. Oh! that last walk in her lovely, holy, gentle life! It led her to her death, but me, at that unknown cost, to life eternal. She certainly gave prudence to the winds. We must have been out three hours, and we found the people in thirty-five houses on that day without a Bible.

"I came home, having seen for the first time how

the poor live; their ignorance, their dirt, their smells —for we went upstairs to more than one sick-room; and I heard my friend, in a way that I had never heard before (though religiously brought up), tell the good news of the love of Jesus to the consumptive and the dying. She spoke to them, but the Spirit of God carried the message home to *me*.

"We finished our walk by a talk with an old woman in a filthy shop, who sold coals and greens, and there I never shall forget the odour; and the old woman was deaf and rude; but we actually turned homewards with thirty-five pence in our bag, and as many names in our collecting book, and as we reached our gate I saw that Elizabeth could scarcely stand.

"She asked leave to go up to her room, and very much to my mother's chagrin was unable to come down to dinner. She was too tired to talk any more that day, and I remember nothing more that afternoon except that when I went to bed at night I took up my Bible to read my usual chapter with a new feeling for it, and a new light upon it from all I had seen and heard that day, and I thought I would begin the Book over again for Elizabeth's sake; and as I read 'Let there be light,' from that hour there was light upon its pages never seen before, for my hard young heart was softened, and a quiet new affection drawn out to this new and gentle friend.

"But in that walk we had both taken fever: mine

proved to be bilious, and hers turned to typhus, and she almost immediately returned home. Before her departure, which was to me a great sorrow, she said she should like me to read the life of Henry Martyn with her, twelve pages a day, to which I gladly agreed; but by the time I had finished it, my new friend and teacher was on earth no more.

"This great grief fixed my resolves. When I recovered, I was allowed, to my own surprise, to go again to the poor people, explain my absence, and once more collect the pence, which, when they amounted to £6, were taken into the Ladies' Bible Committee Meeting at Kennington, of which my grandmother, my father's mother, was at that time president.

"I became in time its minute secretary and cash secretary; always, however, retaining the charge of my own district, which had become to me sacred ground, and always gladly finding time to canvass other districts with any new ladies who required help, which I considered was the duty of an active secretary.

"I remember thinking that the Bible-work was the one work to which I had been called by God, and to which I must keep faithful as one who had been 'baptised for the dead.'"

Here the narrative ends. Ellen White was sixteen when this crisis of her life took place; she was over forty before she wrote "The Book and its

Story;" and forty-eight before what was indeed to be her great life-work was revealed to her. Remember this, young men and maidens, who are bemoaning the hard fate that gives you so little success at nineteen. As for Ellen White, she turned as if by a spiritual instinct towards the road, far, far along which, and all hidden and even unsuspected by her, lay Ellen Ranyard's Bible Woman's Mission.

Many circumstances fostered her devotion to the Book. She became intimate with a large circle of earnest cultivated Christians, among them a man most mighty in the Scriptures, Charles Nice Davies.

Under Mr. Davies' practical teaching, Ellen White grew more and more to enjoy the Bible, and devoted much time both to the reading of the Book herself, and in trying to get others to do so. The Book became to her the very joy of her heart; she was eager that what it was to her it should become to others.

Her love for all who loved the Bible grew naturally with her growing love for the Sacred Word itself, and her loyalty for the Bible Society, which had never flagged since the death of her "dear Elizabeth," became more and more pronounced.

Hers was indeed a noble, broad-souled nature. She was eminently a Catholic Christian, having wide sympathies with all who love and serve Jesus Christ.

In after-life this firm grip of Bible Society principles was of the greatest value to her, and gave its distinctive feature to her mission. It enabled her to work, leaning to no party, but simply striving to lead souls into the fold of the Good Shepherd. Ellen White had a great love for history and archæology, as well as for art and versification. Mr. (afterwards Sir Henry) Layard's discoveries aroused this faculty very vigorously. When the gigantic forms that had so long guarded the buried gateways of buried palaces were brought to England and set up in our own museums, what a thrill they sent through those who regarded them as "stones crying out," messengers from God sent to convince an unbelieving age! And few were more thrilled by them than was Ellen White.

But time had been going by. Her father had left the suburbs of London and settled at Swanscombe, between Gravesend and Dartford, beside a wider, clearer Thames than London's water-way. Ellen White, always an enthusiastic lover of Nature, did not fail to render due homage to Father Thames. He, "the lake-like river," comes into her verses as naturally as do her many brothers and sisters and her parents. Here, at Swanscombe, in a happy, prosperous home, the large family grew up, and gradually dispersed.

Ellen, the good, bright, elder sister, wrote little poems about their marriages, or their other goings away. She had a very happy influence over them, seeking always first of all their souls' good, leading them to love God, the Bible, Nature, all fair, good things, and poetry, especially Wordsworth's.

For Wordsworth she had an extraordinary enthusiasm. The dream of her life was to see him and speak to him. She knew a large part of his poems by heart, and what is more, so wrought upon others of her family, that they too learned many of them. Years afterwards she saw the great master, and conversed with him.

It was not, however, as Ellen White that she was destined to be known to the world. She followed the example of other members of her family, and married Mr. Benjamin Ranyard; but unlike the others, she had no need to leave Swanscombe. She was, she says,

"To a cot I call my own,
Transplanted harp and all;"

yet her new home was quite close to her parents' abode.

She was very busy there writing verses to her children as they came, and many a verse of touching sympathy with friends departed. Several of these poems were afterwards collected and published under the title "Leaves from Life," and the "Border Land, and other Poems." She was already holding mothers' meetings amongst the country poor, and her time was filled up with social duties and the education of her children. It was not till 1852 that it was suggested to her that she should write "The Book and its Story."

Some time before, as a girl of twenty, she had given the world a few of her experiences as a Bible collector. The little book had found a ready sale and many readers. The jubilee of the British and Foreign Bible Society was approaching; Mrs. Ranyard was already well known and greatly valued by the jubilee secretary, the Rev. T. Phillips, who suggested to her that she should write a jubilee volume, telling the Story of the Book and the Story of the Society.

The task involved long and patient labour and much reading; but it was one for which she was very well qualified by many years of daily study and of deepest love for the Book itself. She at length succeeded in putting that story so vividly and yet so simply before her readers that it charmed many of them like a romance.

The reading of "The Book and its Story" marks a new era in many a life now growing old, but young and open to strong impression in 1853, when the Bible Society held its jubilee. Thousands, tens of thousands of homes that book entered to go no more out for ever, to stay there a beloved and honoured friend of the family. Its circulation was enormous.

This literary success, however, was not allowed to disturb the even tenor of Mrs. Ranyard's life. She hated notoriety; any sort of publicity was inconsistent with her ideas of what was feminine. So for many years she stayed in her quiet river-side valley, quite engrossed with her womanly cares, her books, babies, and Bible collecting, the guiding of her household, and the comforting of her ageing parents.

In those long years, hidden away from all except her own circle, she learned in her own dealings with her neighbours what a Bible-woman's work should be; in those long years God was training her day by day for the work He was preparing for her. Little she knew for what purpose the Divine Instructor was fitting her. But as maiden, as wife, as mother, ever since that day in her girlhood when she and Elizabeth Saunders had taken that never-to-be-forgotten walk, Bible-work, in one form or another, but chiefly and continuously in making penny collections among the poor, had been the work to which she felt she had been set apart; and from it she never swerved.

At length there came a time when she and her Mission were to meet. Her boys and girls were growing up, and needed a better education than could be obtained for them in the country. So she and her husband resolved to leave their quiet home and come to London.

They came; they took a house destined to become of historic interest to the friends of a then unthought-of agency for good, a house known now to many thousands by its mission name, "Hunter

Street." Little she thought, when she first wrote her new address, what it would one day grow to mean.

It was in June, 1857, that Mrs. Ranyard, accompanied by a retired physician, who had known London well during his early practice, ventured to take her first walk in the terrible Seven Dials, St. Giles', a locality bad enough even now, in spite of model blocks, schools, mission halls, and new streets, but much worse in those days. Mrs. Ranyard was smitten with horror. Here are a few sentences from her own description of the dismal purlieus of St. Giles'.

"An oppressive, fusty smell assails us as we pass along by the old clothes shops. The dwellers in the cellars beneath the shops are come up this afternoon to breathe the air, the hot and fetid air. The streets are filled with loiterers and loungers. Lazy, dirty women are exhibiting to one another some article of shabby finery, newly revived, which they have just bought. We search in vain among the ragged, sallow children for a bright face or a clean pinafore. There is not a true child-face among them all; nothing speaks of God or Nature but one basket of flowers with which a man happens to be turning the corner of the street.

"Some of the dingy windows of those upper floors are open; and, oh, what dirty, haggard forms are peering out. Many a pane is stuffed with rags, and all around bespeaks a want of light and air and water. We looked up the dark courts and alleys, which had poured forth those squalid children, and which link the seven streets together, and would fain have entered, but there was a something about them which seemed to say, 'Seek no farther, or you may never return.'"

To most persons, after such a glimpse of low London, the most pressing question would be: "How do these dingy swarms of human beings manage to live at all?" But to Mrs. Ranyard's mind there occurred what was to her a still more urgent inquiry: "How are these people in their countless courts and alleys supplied with the Bible?"

She went to Mr. M'Cree, the well-known missionary of St. Giles', and from him she heard that although, thanks to Mr. Thorold, then the Rector of St. Giles' (now Bishop of Rochester and one of the Council of the Bible-woman's Mission), Bibles could be had by penny subscriptions at the church, yet only the decent poor availed themselves of this opportunity.

Mrs. Ranyard felt that no lady, however brave, could be of use among those sunken people; but guided by her own experience as a Bible collector, she asked Mr. M'Cree if he knew a good, poor woman who would venture with a bag of Bibles into every room, as a paid agent for the Bible Society, and who would give a faithful account of her trust.

For all these long years Mrs. Ranyard had been

in training for the mission which was at that very moment just within her reach.

Let us now leave Mrs. Ranyard for a few minutes while we briefly trace the steps by which "Marian B——" became the first Bible-woman.

Marian's parents were in a tolerably respectable position when she was born, but her father was a drunkard, broke his wife's heart, and gradually sank until he and his two daughters were reduced to dwell in a low lodging-house in St. Giles'. He, however, soon died, leaving Marian and her little five-year old sister to get on the best they could. The poor young things had to live in the midst of fearful vice, but, as if by a miracle, they escaped uninjured, although many a night they had to spend on the stairs or the doorsteps to avoid the scenes that were within.

An old man, a fellow-lodger, kind-hearted, although an atheist, took pity on Marian, and taught her to write a little, but told her never to read the Bible. "It is full of lies," he used to say; "you have only to look round you in St. Giles' to see there is no God."

But Marian had a hungry little mind; she managed to pick up reading and knitting by continual gazing in at shop-windows. She never went to any sort of school, and at eighteen married a man as poor as herself. When they went to church to be married she had neither shoes nor stockings, and he had no coat. Her husband, however, poor as he was, was sober, and from that time she knew what it was to have a "home," although that home was humble indeed.

On the 11th of February, 1853, four years before Mrs. Ranyard heard of her, Marian was passing through the streets when it came on to pour with rain. She took shelter in an alley that led up to the little Mission Hall in Dudley Street, where Mr. M'Cree was then preaching. Hearing a voice, Marian went in to listen. The address was nearly ended; but some verses quoted from the eleventh of Hebrews touched Marian's heart. She knew that the book always used in mission halls was the Bible, and that those words must be in the Bible.

When the address was over, the preacher announced that a lending library had just been formed, and that on the following evening books would be lent to the poor. This was good news for Marian. She was at the hall early, and was the first applicant. She had intended to borrow "Uncle Tom's Cabin," which was then creating an enormous interest in every class of society, but a strong impulse that she could not resist impelled her to ask for a Bible instead. It was as if she had heard a voice whispering to her, "Do not borrow Uncle Tom, borrow a Bible." So she asked for one.

"A Bible!" exclaimed the missionary; "we did not mean to lend Bibles; but wait, I will fetch you one. It is a token for good that the Book of God, the Best of Books, should be the first one asked for, and lent from this place."

He brought her the Bible, and asked if he should call and read a chapter with her. She said respectfully, "No, sir, thank you; we are very quiet folk, my husband might not like it; I will take the book and read it for myself."

In the letter Mr. M'Cree had in his pocket when Mrs. Ranyard spoke to him, Marian had written: "I asked you to lend me a Bible; you knew not my name or residence, yet with cheerful kindness you complied with that request; and, for the first time in my life, I brought a Bible into my home. That Bible I still retain; of its influence over me none but its great Author can be aware; nor of the slow but certain means by which its precious truths have been revealed to my hitherto benighted soul."

Marian was then eking out her husband's little earnings by cutting fire-papers, or moulding waxflowers, or making bags for silversmiths, but in spite of poverty and work, she found she had two or three hours a day that she could spare, and in that letter which was in Mr. M'Cree's pocket when Mrs. Ranyard spoke to him, she had told him that she had received such mercy from God that she had devoted every moment of her life to prove her gratitude. "I have thought over many plans," she wrote, "all of which I have dismissed but one, which is for me perfectly practicable; and it is to ask your co-operation in it that I presume to address you.

"During the time I was in the hospital I had frequent opportunities of witnessing the utterly friendless condition of many poor outcasts, the plight of their persons and clothing proving their need of a female hand. Now I wish to dedicate the time I have to spare not so much to the decent poor, who have a claim upon the sympathy of their neighbours, but to the lost and degraded of my own sex. No matter how degraded she may be, it will be enough for me that she require my aid, such as washing her, and repairing her garments."

This was the substance of the long letter which the missionary read to Mrs. Ranyard. He said it was perfectly genuine, and "like the writer when you knew her."

Mrs. Ranyard was convinced that this was the kind of person she sought, and that if she could carry the message from God to every door, opportunities of many forms of usefulness might arise. She made an offer to Marian, and Marian accepted it with delight. She wrote:

"I believe that grace that was able to subdue my own heart will never leave me in my effort to pour into the hearts of others that blessed Message. I am myself too strong a proof of the power of Almighty God to dare to doubt in any case the mercy which broke down the strongholds of sin in me."

To penetrate the dens of Soho and Seven Dials, not to give away tickets for bread and coals, but to ask people to pay for Bibles at a penny a week, would have seemed a most visionary scheme to many good Christians had they been told of it. But they were not told of it. Very little was said to any one about the attempt until its success more than justified its seeming audacity.

It was indeed terrible work; but it was also most blessed. Marian, although she had lived in St. Giles' for thirty-three years, soon found that its hidden recesses were unknown to her. Even she, used as she was to the neighbourhood, was surprised at the state of things she discovered by her room to room visits. Some of her earliest visits were to courts where no one so much as professed to get an honest living, where every one was "tarred with the same brush," and a very black brush too; where dwellings were worse than the cow-houses of these days, with a heap of filthy straw for a bed; where hare and rabbit skins were kept until the stench of them bred fever; where one pump or tap, with a very scanty supply of water, had to serve the whole court.

Yet into these places the Bible-woman went; often repulsed, it is true, but more frequently treated with respect; for the lowest, although they knew nothing of the Book, had a notion it was something intended to do people good. One "lady with lettuces" even went so far as to make a curtsey to Marian for the sake of the Book she carried.

In only one court was she badly treated, when a bucket of filth was emptied on her from an upper window. This at once made nearly the whole population her friends. One woman took her in and wiped her bonnet, and another brought water to wash her face, and were afterwards among her warmest protectors.

But how about the actual sale? Were any Bibles sold after all? At the end of the first month seventy Bible subscribers were on the books. The taste then was for small copies with gilt edges. Now it is for the large print two-shilling Bible. Under the circumstances seventy subscribers was certainly a much larger number than Mrs. Ranyard's most sanguine hopes had anticipated.

This result of the first month's work cheered Mrs. Ranyard exceedingly. She began to think that perhaps the missing link between the very lowest of our people and our upper classes had been found; she began to suspect that the Bible-woman was that missing link.

Much knowledge as to how the poor live was secured by Marian's visits, which were daily reported to Mrs. Ranyard; "but," says Mrs. Ranyard, "that was not the first aim. The enterprise was undertaken only with a deep sense that the Message from God should be carried to every member of the human family."

Before the end of her second month's visiting, Marian gave her now historical tea-party to eight women who were her most punctual subscribers. Some were buyers of hare and rabbit skins, some sellers of watercresses, fruit, fish, or flowers; but all had bad husbands. Marian had chairs for five of them; the rest sat on the side of her bed. She was not extravagant in providing for them, one ounce of tea, half a pound of lump sugar, half a pound of butter, and a quartern loaf being all that was required. They all brought their new Bibles with them. Marian talked to them, simply telling them what that Book had done for her; and that *that* was the reason she was so glad to bring it to them.

It was a simple entertainment, but they were all encouraged to talk about themselves, and so when they parted they all declared they had never spent such a happy evening before. As for Marian herself, she declared that every week's work seemed happier and happier.

At the end of twenty weeks she had sold one hundred and thirty Bibles and one hundred and twenty Testaments, and mostly to those who would not have bought them from any one else. She generally made friends of her subscribers, so that she now found a welcome in over two hundred rooms.

Mrs. Ranyard and her one Bible-woman soon found out that many things besides Bibles were needed. They sold for a halfpenny a printed recipe of a "nourishing soup that could be made for sixpence," and they lent a saucepan to make it in. They started a clothing club and a sewing meeting; they thought and planned for individual cases in all sorts of ways. Thus, little by little, there grew up a Domestic as well as a Bible mission.

In the simplest faith in the power of the Sword of the Spirit, and with intense womanly sympathy, joined to great sagacity and strong common sense, Mrs. Ranyard gradually worked her way. The means she used for getting at the objects of her loving care were singularly well adapted for their work, and the results were so satisfactory that after a few months of trial, Mrs. Ranyard, who was then editing a periodical called "The Book and its Mission," ventured to describe her St. Giles' work in its pages.

Many of the poor creatures whom "Marian" tried to help were Irish; and an Irish friend, one of the readers of Mrs. Ranyard's little magazine, was so deeply interested by the account of this poor woman's devotion to *her* Irish, that she sent, unasked, a donation of £5. This was the first private donation to funds that have by this time amounted to very many thousands of pounds. The Bible Society had, however, given help before.

Mrs. Ranyard had a wonderfully graphic and earnest way of describing the scenes among which Marian worked. A large circle of readers soon became intensely interested in her doings. Here and there those who had long grieved over the dark places of London began to ask, Why not multiply "Marians"? The record of the different missions as they sprang up all over London fills by this time many volumes.

Mrs. Ranyard soon found it advisable to entirely devote her magazine to furthering her mission. She called it "The Missing Link," meaning by that term the Bible-woman, the missing link between the poorest and the upper classes.

In our limited space it is quite impossible to give even a sketch of this constantly growing work of which Mrs. Ranyard was for twenty-two years the great organising brain; suffice it to say that, beginning with one Bible-woman, there were over one hundred and seventy when Mrs. Ranyard was taken from them, and that these women, for Bibles and clothing, had received from the very poor more than £130,000, a very large percentage of which would inevitably have been spent in drink had not the Bible and Domestic Mission diverted it from its evil course; for, as one woman told Marian when she was collecting sixpences for cheap beds, "Nineteen out of twenty of those sixpences would have gone for gin," to which many around responded, "Ay, that they would!"

The "Mothers' Meeting," now a recognised part of the weekly services of nearly every place of worship, grew out of this mission. Who can tell the blessing it has been to thousands of poor mothers?

For eleven years the Bible-women worked on alone, but the appalling need of *trained nurses* for the sick poor becoming more and more urgent, the Bible-woman Nurse was added to the Mission Staff.

Mrs. Ranyard had to set about training her nurses herself. Not without difficulty did she procure their admission into the medical and surgical wards of hospitals; but she left behind her when she was taken home about eighty nurses who attend the sick poor in their own homes, visiting seven thousand persons in the course of a year, taking with them the beef-tea or cereal food it is so often impossible for the patients to have properly cooked in their own wretched rooms.

"Oh," they often say, "Nurse does make gruel so nice and smooth! Not lumpy like! Made with milk too!"

These nurses are indeed a real blessing. Their reports are most touching, and, alas! most terribly true.

Mrs. Ranyard held the strings of the whole Mission in her own hand. "I give you a good long line," she used to tell her people with her pleasant humorous smile, "but remember I've a hook at the end. I can always pull you in." But while perfectly mistress of the situation, she had the most profound humility, and was willing to learn from the humblest worker.

She was from first to last profoundly impressed

with the everlasting importance of the Word of God. Her industry was wonderful. She was at work by four or five in the morning while her health held out; and even during her last illness she would be awake then, reading letters from the Bible-women or preparing reports for her Magazine. Two great sorrows fell upon her closing life. Her girls, each of them, when they reached their eighteenth year, were taken from her. She had looked forward so much to their help and sympathy; their young lives opened with so much sweetness and promise that, although she strove to resign them not only with patience to God's will, but, as the elder, Edith, said to her just before she died, to "rejoice in it," the repeated blows left scars upon her most tender, motherly heart that were never quite healed.

She wrote right up to the last. The Reading Room of the British Museum was her refuge. Her early love for Biblical archæology never waned; nor indeed did any love of hers ever die out. She had a tenacity of grasp for a person or a principle once held that was indeed stronger than death. She had a great diversity of gifts; the most precious was her strange power of winning affection, and that from people of the most various kinds. She was very sweet and bright and witty at home; she had the hearts of all her workers; her sympathy, her tact, her trust in them were wonderful, but no one took a liberty with her. All were anxious that she should be satisfied and thankful when she was so. She is "dear Mrs. Ranyard" still to all who survive.

As she approached her threescore years and ten, her health and strength gradually failed. She toiled on still "amid deepening shadows, amid weariness, dimness of eye, and failing hand in the severely noble temper of Christian humility, unconscious of self," until at last absolute illness forced self-consciousness upon her.

In the February of 1879, her seventieth year, she had a severe bronchial attack, but she fought through it with characteristic resolution. Her friends and she herself thought she was recovering; she rose and seemed cheerful; then the end came swiftly, and her busy life on earth was over.

Great was the mourning and weeping when they carried her body to its last resting-place. One present writes "how they wept for her, the founder of Bible-women to the poor women of London; the friend who had gathered alms for them, gifts of money, food and raiment, gifts of flowers and fruit; the friend who had cared for them in their sickness and sorrow, who had sent nurses to them in their own homes, the friend who had cared for the souls of their poor mothers, sent God's Word to them, and teachers to show the way of salvation, and tell them of the love of Christ. Our dear Bible teacher is dead. Her voice is hushed, her pen laid aside, her loving heart still."

But her work lives—lives and grows. Its new

home is the house in Adelphi Terrace, through the windows of which one sees Cleopatra's Needle and the great crowded bend of the broad-water of Thames, and under the title of "Bible Work" (Cassell and Company) the chronicles of the Mission are still month by month continued.

(*Our Portrait is from a Photograph by W. and A. H. Fry, Brighton.*)

www.ingramcontent.com/pod-product-compliance
Lightning Source LLC
Chambersburg PA
CBHW030402170426
43202CB00010B/1460